BOOK OF
DONAIR

Everything you wanted to know about the
Halifax food that became Canada's favourite kebab

Lindsay Wickstrom

MacIntyre Purcell Publishing Inc.
194 Hospital Rd.
Lunenburg, Nova Scotia
B0J 2C0
(902) 640-3350

www.macintyrepurcell.com
info@macintyrepurcell.com

Printed and bound in Canada by Friesens

Cover design: Denis Cunningham
Book design: Denis Cunningham
Front cover photo: Vernon Oickle (Taken at A-1 Pizza in Liverpool, N.S.)
Author photo (back cover): Lynne Fox

ISBN: 978-1-77276-154-2

Library and Archives Canada Cataloguing in Publication Title: Book of donair : everything you wanted to know about the Halifax food that became Canada's   favourite kebab / Lindsay Wickstrom. Names: Wickstrom, Lindsay, author. Identifiers: Canadiana 20200226983 | ISBN 9781772761542 (softcover) Subjects: LCSH: Skewer cooking—Nova Scotia—Halifax Regional Municipality. | LCSH: Cooking—Nova   Scotia—Halifax Regional Municipality. | LCSH: Cooking, Canadian—Maritime Provinces style. Classification: LCC TX834 .W53 2020 | DDC 641.7/6—dc23

MacIntyre Purcell Publishing Inc. would like to acknowledge the financial support of the Government of Canada and the Nova Scotia Department of Tourism, Culture and Heritage.

Funded by the Government of Canada | Canadä   NOVA SCOTIA

Dedicated to Peter Gamoulakos and to all of the donair warriors who came after him.

Donair Timeline

· **1830-1870:** Invention of the vertical rotating spit and the döner kebab.

· **1920s:** The döner kebab is brought to Greece (where it will become the gyros) by refugees from Asia Minor.

· **1965:** The first gyro is served in the United States.

· **1972:** The first döner kebab is sold in Germany.

· **1974:** Peter Gamoulakos serves the first donair in Canada at Velos Souvlakia (Bedford, N.S.)

· **1976:** Peter Gamoulakos opens the first Mr. Donair restaurant. Five more locations (including Quinpool Rd.) will open that year.

· **1977:** Mr. Donair becomes King of Donair.

— In New Brunswick, the Greco chain of restaurants is established. Greco's sister company (later known as Bonté Foods), will become a national leader in donair production and distribution.

· **1979:** King of Donair is sold to Nick Garonis and Takis Mitropoulos.

· **1982:** Charles Smart opens the first donair restaurant and production facility in Edmonton.

· **1985:** Mr. Donair Ltd. (a donair production facility) is established by Peter Gamoulakos, with his brother, John Kamoulakos.

· **1987:** European Food Shop opens on the corner of Blowers and Grafton, followed by Sicilian Pizza and King of Donair. This marks the birth of Halifax's iconic Pizza Corner.

· **1989:** Sam Nahas buys the rights to King of Donair.

· **1991:** Peter Gamoulakos dies.

· **1994:** Leo Toulany starts making donair meat in Timberlea, N.S. He will grow the business (now called "Leo's Donair") to become a leading distributor of donair cones in the Halifax Regional Municipality.

· **1995:** Sam Tawachi opens Athena Donair in Edmonton, a federally inspected donair manufacturing plant.

· **1996:** King of Donair adopts the electric shaving knife.

· **1997:** Glen Petitpas creates the first known Halifax donair web page.

· **2001:** Halifax King of Donair Soccer Team wins the Canadian National Soccer Championships.

· **2003:** Nick Garonis retires from the donair business after opening the King of Donair in Lower Sackville, N.S.

· **2005:** John Kamoulakos sells Mr. Donair Ltd. to Tony's Meats of Antigonish, N.S.

· **2006:** A series of food poisonings in Edmonton are traced to donair consumption.

· **2008:** The Federal-Provincial-Territorial Donair Working Group releases food safety guidelines for donair and shawarma in Canada.

· **2012:** The King of Donair on Pizza Corner closes its doors.

· **2014:** Anthony Bourdain tries a donair at the Devour Food Film Festival in Wolfville, N.S.

· **2015:** The donair is declared the official food of Halifax.

· **2018:** King of Donair expands to Western Canada.

· **2020:** The first book ever written about the donair is published. (You are here!)

A donair at Sicilian Pizza on Blowers & Grafton (Pizza Corner).

1

Canada's Kebab

East Coast Lifestyle

"I look for unique foods, unique to the region. It is your most famous, it is the signature dish… like the New York dirty water hot dog, we love it. We don't apologize for it."
– Anthony Bourdain (1)

The year was 2015. The city of Halifax had declared the donair its official food, after an inconclusive 43-page staff report and a tie-breaker vote by Mayor Mike Savage. The outcome may seem obvious to some, dubious to others, but this little piece of history was indeed dripping in controversy.

There were those who didn't want council wasting our precious tax dollars on a street food study, when transportation, housing and food security ought to be on the front of the menu. Other critics felt the donair was an embarrassment to the fair city of Halifax and the refinement of our collective palate. "Why not lobster?" was a common retort, as if lobster is unique to Halifax, and our crustaceous rolls somehow rival those of Maine and Connecticut.

Yet Nova Scotia tends to get pigeonholed as "Lobsters and Lighthouses" in brochure tourism. We play up our Celtic culture (at the expense of our Mi'kmaq, Acadian, German, African-Nova Scotian, and later-arriving cultures) and tend to neglect anything that isn't on brand.

The donair has been our dirty little secret. We point the tourists toward restaurants endowed with lobster traps and buoys, while we sneak away to eat greasy meat slathered in a sticky, sweet sauce.

One day there were no donairs. The next day they seemed to be everywhere. They had spread to Cape Breton and New Brunswick with very little fanfare. The donair became a fixture of Maritime life; it was just there, alongside pizza, which itself had been introduced to the province only a decade earlier, in the 1960s, but was already entrenched in the fabric of everyday life.

YOU HAVE EXPLAINED WHAT DONAIRS ARE TO PEOPLE THAT ARE NOT FROM HERE.

We would emerge as zombies from the over-serving nightclubs, making our pilgrimage to Pizza Corner, that sacred corner of grease and carbs. We would sit on the stone wall in front of the church, legs spread, heads hanging, in this shameful ritual. We'd leave behind a trail of carnage: milky pools and spicy debris.

Then we'd all stumble hopefully home, for dreamless black sleeps with still sticky lips. The seagulls would descend for cleanup, their shadows enhanced by dim streetlights, as they overtook the corner like apocalyptic horsemen.

Wayward wanderers would discreetly slip into their quarters, telephoning delivery demons and waking up with tinfoil companions cradled in their arms.

Donairs were not for the lucky-in-love, but the recourse of the degenerate. They were the butt of toilet humour, the scapegoat of indigestion.

The "mystery meat" with the "secret sauce" was wrapped in urban legend. It was so commonplace that we took it for granted, no more significant than hamburgers or spaghetti. We didn't realize that it was ours.

It wasn't until we made westward pilgrimages to Ontario or Alberta, for school or work, that the donair became a symbol of home.

The donair was the recourse of the homesick, comforting and familiar. We would get family to ship deconstructed donairs from our favourite shops to the oil field, to weddings, to war zones. Maritimers would connect on internet forums, sharing their recipes or directions to rogue pizza shops serving the delicacy in unlikely locales. Wholesale businesses opened, shipping Maritime staples to the rest of Canada.

This happened in waves over several decades, with the ebbs and flows of busts and booms. Over time, the momentum of shared experience started to build, culminating in one big wave of collective pride.

The donair was somewhere in the symbolic epicentre of the East Coast lifestyle. We just didn't realize it. We didn't think the world would love our true nature. How could our neglected province, with its damp and foggy coastline, hanging onto Canada's fringes by a tiny isthmus, and characterized by its "casserole culture" by bad faith journalists, produce one of the few, truly original street foods in Canada?

The Upper Canadians would say: "Isn't it just a gyro?"

Nothing special. Nothing to see here, folks!

It had been 42 years since the first donair was sold, and it had largely been taken for granted. Until now. Oh, the year was two thousand and fifteen. I was told we'd cruise the scene, for a sociable pub, we'd pay no cover, eat some grease. God damn them all….

Donair Wasteland

"I have a fond memory of my dad actually FedExing donairs they grew up on to my aunt in Guelph. Luckily, they're becoming easier to find across this delicious country."
– Brittany Toole (from CBC, 2017) (2)

Glen Petitpas moved away from Timberlea, N.S. in 1995 to start grad school at McMaster University. When he got to Hamilton, Ont., he noticed the complete absence of donairs.

"I looked all over Hamilton and found a place that sold something. It was a pita place that claimed to have a donair but the dressing was like ranch dressing and it had lettuce and pickles. I was quite shocked. It was really unpleasant." (3)

Eventually he was able to procure a recipe from someone who used to work in a donair shop. It would take him four hours to make the meat, kneading it until his hands were sore, and freezing it in batches. If he ran out of meat, he would sometimes buy a plain gyro, take it home, and add his homemade donair sauce. He called it a "tolerable donair replacement." (3)

Worried that he would misplace his treasured recipes, Glen decided to create a permanent online resource, for himself and others, to access the blueprints.

r/halifax
u/Socialjustcewarfarin • ld

Flying to Toronto anytime soon? Bring me a Donair and I'll pick you up at the airport and drop you off.

`Question`

• Yes I'm serious
• No I'm not a murderer
• YYZ or YTZ

A desperate plea for donairs, from the donair wasteland of Toronto.

To his surprise, he started getting thank you e-mails from ex-pat Maritimers around the world. People would share their own recipes with him, and tips on the whereabouts of authentic donairs across Canada, all of which he would post on his untitled website with the curious "harvard.edu" URL. It may be the oldest donair fan site on the internet, dating to at least 1997.

Glen Petitpas

"I know at the time if you googled 'donair recipe' the closest you got was a 'donair kebab' recipe from someone called Derek Stapleton," Glen tells me. "I still have the original (broken) link on my donair page as tribute."

Today, Glen works for the Harvard-Smithsonian Center for Astrophysics. "My most current research is studying the molecular gas (physical conditions and dynamics) at the centres of galaxies, with the occasional dip into the world of high redshift and ultraluminous infrared galaxies." [4]
… and donairs.

Glen's story is symptomatic of a larger movement. There were many homesick Maritimers wanting a taste of nostalgia. That was clear. But the donair was harder to sell to our neighbours, who hadn't acquired a taste for our strange, sweet sauce, and didn't understand how to eat a pita wrap that defied the very act of being picked up and eaten.

There have been many franchise and distribution attempts targeting Ontario, Quebec and Maine, which have been mostly unsuccessful. Getting Upper Canadians and Americans to eat donairs has been a hard sell.

"They're really not that pleasant the first time you have them," Glen says. "Most people, after their first try, think they're terrible." [3]

The Renaissance

"While nobody was paying attention, food quietly assumed the place in youth culture that used to be occupied by rock 'n' roll – individual, fierce and intensely political."
– Jonathan Gold (5)

When the recession hit in 2008, everything changed. Fine dining made way for the upscale casual and gourmet comfort foods, coinciding with the coming-of-age of food- and tech-obsessed millennials.

A pair of donairs at Hopgood's Foodliner in Toronto, which closed in 2017. (Photo: David Laurence)

Food became more accessible and more "hip". This led to an era of pop-ups, food trucks, and street food, the "authentic", "local" and "extreme". Before we knew it, we had *Epic Meal Time* wrapping everything in bacon, and Instagram influencers with their constant stream of unicorn frappuccinos and rainbow bagels.

It was only a matter of time before someone made a donair doughnut.

Our stigmatized dirty drunk food was suddenly being celebrated by gourmands with innovative twists. People started seeing the donair as a truly Canadian food that emerged out of a unique historical and cultural context; it was something to be set before Guy Fieri or Anthony Bourdain.

Donair Doughnuts from Robie St. Station in collaboration with Tony's Donair. (Photo: Dagley Media).

By 2012, Chef Geoff Hopgood was selling pairs of taco-sized donairs on a paper bag "plate" for $12 at his trendy restaurant in Toronto's Roncesvalles Village. The pitas were baked in-house daily. The meat, a puree of beef and pork, was cooked sous vide before being shaved off a spit and griddled to order, topped with Ontario hothouse tomatoes, and finely diced vidalia onions.

Meanwhile, Edmonton's High Voltage was serving "the first international flavour donairs" like Caribbean jerk and blue cheese. They sprinkled their dainty pita wraps with sea salt and herbs before grilling them on a panini press.

In 2014, Field Guide opened in Halifax, serving seasonally inspired sharing dishes. Their signature dish is none other than a donair, disguised as a trendy Asian bao. Fancy-pants donairs even made a brief appearance in New York City in 2015, when King Bee, an Acadian-inspired restaurant (now closed), started serving a brunch donair, served optionally with a fried egg (New York Magazine dubbed it an "Acadian Gyro"). (6)

That summer Halifax had its first Donair Crawl. Organizer Amy Langdon had no stake in the donair biz; she was just a health-care administrator who happened to love donairs.

Donair steamed bun at Field Guide (Photo: Michelle Doucette).

The inaugural 2015 Halifax Donair Crawl. (Photo: Dagley Media).

She told Global News: "I was hungry one night and I asked where was the best place in the city to get a donair. I had a ton of responses and my friend said 'it sounds like you're planning a donair crawl'. It just kind of stuck with me, and I threw the idea out there and this is it." (7)

It was a grassroots event, thrown together over the course of a month, but Amy managed to get sponsorship, T-shirts, and proceeds going to charity.

There was even a donair doughnut.

Event organizer: Amy Langdon
(Photo: Dagley Media).

As the crowd descended on Quinpool Road, a thoroughfare and shopping district west of the Halifax Common, there was a sense of community and pride. Moreover, there was the sense that something was shifting. We were out in broad daylight feasting on what critics claimed was a "dirty food", best left to the secrecy of the witching hours and the oblivion of intoxication. Yet here we were in all our glory, claiming ownership of our little piece of the world.

It's Official

"Here we are a week into 2015, and donair is everywhere. Montreal has a donair shop now, donair is slowly taking over Fort Mac, and even Vancouver has donair on the mind. Therefore, we're declaring 2015 the Year of Donair."
- Michael Dinn, on donair.org

"Edmonton is the true donair champion, the true mecca of donairs," Omar Mouallem said, boldly concluding his presentation at Edmonton's PechaKucha Night 2014. A PechaKucha is a storytelling art, originating in Japan, where 20 slides are presented with 20 seconds of commentary each. It's an efficient, creative and personal way for people to share their work with the community.

Omar's work was journalism. He went on to write an in-depth piece for the *Walrus* about the history of the donair in Alberta. That year he also wrote donair articles for *Maclean's* and *Swerve Magazine*. In 2017, he wrote a piece for *Canadian Geographic*'s Canada 150 special issue, which officially made the donair one of CanGeo's "150 icons of Canada". A local paper had deemed Omar "Edmonton's Foremost Donair Scholar".

It may surprise some Nova Scotians to learn that Albertans have been happily eating donairs since the early 1980s. They were introduced by migrant labourers from the East Coast, and have independently evolved, with their own unique style and attitude.

"There was no official attempt to make it Edmonton's official dish," Omar told me, via FaceTime.

"For the people who weren't at that event and didn't see the performance, I think they took it a little too literally. For the people live tweeting it, I think the satire, irony, cheekiness got lost in that, and a couple blogs started talking about it more sincerely than I intended."

The next thing he knew, it was being discussed on CBC Edmonton's morning show: "What is Edmonton's official dish?"

"So," I followed up, "*you* are indirectly responsible for the donair becoming the official food of Halifax?"

He responded with a cheeky smirk and an evasive shrug.

"Your councillor got a little overprotective about this, but to see my work referenced in a civic document, it amuses me to no end. Don't let anyone tell you that you can't change the world!"

We both agreed that Edmonton's true dish is the green onion cake. There has been an unsuccessful movement since 2013 to make it the city's official dish.

Omar's PechaKucha presentation was in March of 2014, and by October of 2015, Halifax regional council voted 12-4 in favour of a staff report to consider the donair as a candidate for the official food. Coun. Linda Mosher said she was worried that Edmonton might lay claim to it.

"I'm not asking for a big report," Mosher told her fellow councillors, according to a CBC story. "I don't want this to be costly, but I think that this is unique to Halifax. It was invented here and it's ours and they're already calling it our official food."

Coun. Bill Karsten argued: "Donairs have been served in Turkey and Syria and countries abroad for centuries. Different version, but a donair nonetheless."

"If we don't do this, won't we all falafel?" Coun. Tim Outhit reportedly chimed in.

Mayor Mike Savage adjourned the discussion: "I don't want to see any sauce on that report when it comes back." (8)

The staff report came back two months later. Its 43 pages cited articles from *National Geographic*, *The Globe and Mail*, tourism advertisements, a song by local rapper Classified, and even a quote from Anthony Bourdain, who had tried his first donair at the previous year's Devour Food Film Festival.
The report was inconclusive.

"In the absence of detailed staff analysis, including consideration of supporting processes to identify and evaluate other official foods or other official features, staff would not put forward a recommendation for a proclamation. It is at Council's discretion to direct a proclamation by the Mayor."

Coun. Waye Mason translated this for me as: "Do it if you want, folks, we ain't touching it!"

This Archie comic was released as a special edition for Hal Con 2014, and was included in Halifax regional council's staff report as "evidence" that the donair is an iconic food of the city.

"If Council wishes to proceed," the report said, "a member of Council may move that Halifax Regional Council authorize and direct that the Mayor make a proclamation declaring the donair the official food of Halifax."

And he did.

On December 8th, 2015, the donair was declared the official food of Halifax.

I asked Waye Mason about this, and he boiled it down to "silly season" at City Hall (it was almost exactly a year away from the 2016 election). "Folks start to bring forward feel-good motions, local issues, things that will get noticed."

Mason had voted against the motion, citing better uses for tax dollars, but later tweeted that he had a donair for dinner that very night.

At a 2018 PechaKucha in Edmonton, Omar Mouallem addressed the rivalry he may have stirred up between Edmonton and Halifax donair claims:

"The dish is more than just a regional sensation. Like the butter tart, it has its origins in a specific part of the country but it's come to symbolize more than Ontario's questionable and perverse love of raisins. Inside this mystery meat … is Canada's multicultural heart and soul. To really appreciate the uniqueness of Canada's great cuisine you must understand the rotating kebab's history – how it evolved across the world's continents before it took form as a spicy meat bomb wrapped up with a creamy sweet sauce in a tender pita.

"My fellow citizens, I'm afraid there are no number of donairs we can consume in this great city of ours to top the zealotry (of Halifax) so I concede it's not our official food. No, it's Canada's."

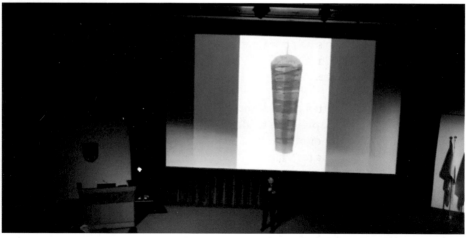

Omar Mouallem presents 'Kebabs: A Global Phenomenon' at Pecha Kucha Nights Edmonton at NAIT's Shaw Theatre on March 16, 2018. (From YouTube).

2

It All Began with the Döner Kebab

The World's First Cooks

"Eat it like a caveperson. Tell no one."
– Ferhat Dirik (co-owner of Mangal 2 in London, U.K.) (9)

Wonderwerk Cave in South Africa has housed humans for two million years, and it was here in 2012 that archeologists found the site of the earliest known barbecue. When examining sediment from inside the cave, they found remnants of a million-year-old campfire with traces of carbonized twigs, leaves and animal bones. (10) This would seem to suggest that our ancestors had learned how to control fires enough to get one going in a cave kitchen. We now have strong evidence that humans have been cooking for at least a million years.

Back then, it would have been our ancestors, *homo erectus*, who had brains twice the size of any of their predecessors, thanks to learning how to cook. (11)

Cooking made meat and plants easier to chew and digest, more readily absorbed and much more nourishing. Surplus calories were suddenly available to power up hungry brains. Instead of spending the whole day grinding and gnashing at roots and cartilage, the busy schedules of *homo erectus* had opened up for … finding better ways to cook more delicious things! (11)

There is something wholesome and primal about cooking over fire. We still enjoy sitting around a campfire with meat on sticks, staring into the flames, while carefully rotating our tubes of mechanically separated animals over the embers.

Shhh… Kebab!

In North America we are familiar with the family-friendly shish-kebab: grilled wooden skewers of meats and vegetables that became all the rage at backyard barbecues in the 1960s. I also have fond memories of my mom's fruit kebabs at birthday parties, and I

Photo of shishliki. (Photo: Amy Jo Ehman, author of Out of Old Saskatchewan Kitchens).

would never have guessed that this was a quirky take on Mediterranean food, very likely a "party idea" in *Canadian Living* magazine circa 1992.

Let's now trace our way back from the *Canadian Living* recipe section to the *Kitab al-Tabikh*, a medieval cookbook of Mesopotamian, Persian and Arab cuisine, in which there are descriptions of "kebab" as cut-up meats cooked over flame. (12) It is often said that it started with Persian soldiers on war campaigns (or the troops of Alexander the Great), cooking meat on their swords over the communal fire.

But archeologists have excavated portable barbecues of clay and stone near the sites of ancient Mycenaean palaces, fitted to hold skewers over hot coals. It turns out the Greeks were already having tailgate parties as much as 3,000 years ago! (13)

Regardless of all the difficult-to-prove origin myths, we do know that the Ottoman Empire played an instrumental role in the spread of the kebab. Şiş kebap ("sword" or "skewer" kebab) is what we in North America call "shish". For all intents and purposes, "kebab" means "grilled meat" and it originated somewhere in the Middle East.

Today, skewered and grilled meats are found all over the world: chicken satay in Southeast Asia, souvlaki in Greece, yakitori in Japan, shashlik in Russia, and Brazilian barbecue are just a few examples.

Everyone loves a shish kebab, but what does any of this have to do with the donair? Well, it all started with a special kind of kebab. It all started with the döner kebab.

You Spin Me Right 'Round, Baby

Donair, doner, donner, doener, döner: these are all spellings for what is more or less the same dish. Properly speaking, it is *döner* and it originates from Turkey. It seems to be pronounced differently based on the region and speaker, but some pronunciations sound an awful lot like "donair".

So, we know that "kebab" means "grilled meat", but what does "*döner*" mean? It's time to start unravelling the tinfoil!

It may surprise you to learn that the word "*döner*" simply means "to turn" or "to rotate" from the Old Turkish word "*dönmek*". Therefore, *döner kebab* essentially means "rotating grilled meat". (14)

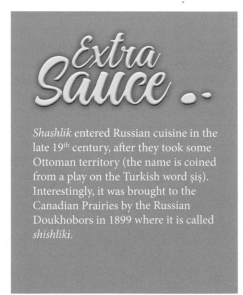

Shashlik entered Russian cuisine in the late 19th century, after they took some Ottoman territory (the name is coined from a play on the Turkish word şiş). Interestingly, it was brought to the Canadian Prairies by the Russian Doukhobors in 1899 where it is called *shishliki*.

This is thought to be the earliest known photograph of döner kebab, and attributed to English photographer James Robertson in 1855.

Despite the literal meaning of *döner kebab*, it wasn't mere rotation that made this kebab revolutionary. It was vertical rotation. The inception of the *döner kebab* happened alongside the invention of the vertical rotating spit. Prior to this, the horizontal rotisserie was the preferred method. The çağ kebabi, a horizontally spitted roast of lamb over wood fire, is thought to be the predecessor of the *döner kebab*, and today remains an iconic dish of Erzurum, Turkey.

Whereas horizontal kebabs allow dripping fats to ignite and singe the meat, vertical rotisseries keep the heat source off to the side, allowing the juices to bathe the meat from top to bottom.

Most accounts say the vertical rotisserie was invented around 1870 by Iskender Effendy in Bursa, Turkey. But according to some historians of Turkish folk culture, Hamdi Usta of Kastamonu was the true inventor, around 1830. (15)(16) This would appear to be corroborated by what is thought to be the first photograph of a *döner kebab*, dated 1855, which, at the very least, shows that *döner kebab* has been around longer than the Iskender claim.

In Turkey, where there are many types of kebab, it is usually just called *döner*, and this refers to the thinly shaved, rotisserie meat (lamb and beef are most common). It is traditionally served with rice and salad. Served in bread, it is simply called *ekmek arası döner* (*döner* in between bread) but there are a few distinct preparations as well:

Döner Dürüm: Döner meat wrapped in lavash or yufka (flatbreads).

Tombik (or gobit kebab): The "chubby" sandwich, using a bun-shaped pita.

Iskender Kebab at Turkish Delight in Halifax

Iskender Kebab: This preparation consists of *döner* meat plated on top of cut up *pide* bread (leavened Turkish flat bread) and topped with yogurt, melted butter and tomato sauce. It is Iskender's namesake dish, and is still served at *Kebapçı İskender*, which is now run by his descendants.

Shawarma: The Middle Eastern Legacy

Thanks to Ottoman imperialism, the *döner kebab* spread around the world. It became the *shawarma* in the Middle East in the 19th century, and is widely eaten in Lebanon, Syria, Egypt, Palestine, Iraq and beyond.

The word "shawarma" comes from another Turkish word for "turning": çevirme. Since there is no "ch" sound in Arabic, the word became "shawarma".

Its wrap form is generally distinguished by its marinated meats, Arabic (pocket) pita, and pickled vegetables.

A standard Lebanese-Canadian shawarma looks something like this:

Chicken shawarma from Mezza Lebanese Kitchen (Facebook)

The Meat:
Cuts of marinated lamb, beef, or chicken stacked onto a vertical rotisserie.

The Bread:
Arabic pita, which is sometimes opened and stuffed.

The Toppings:
Any combination of tomato, cucumber, parsley, onion, pickled vegetables, French fries, chili sauce, tahini (sesame) or *toum* (garlic) sauce.

Shawarma has its regional differences around the world. It can be a simple preparation of meat, pickles and French fries or it can feature a smorgasbord of salads and condiments.

Israeli-style: Lamb, or dark turkey meat, layered with lamb fat served in a pocket of laffa bread with French fries. Some shops will top it with a single falafel ball. Tahini and hummus are used instead of dairy-based sauces due to religious dietary restrictions. There are a variety of other toppings and sauces that can be added, such as: pickled mango sauce, chili sauce, roasted eggplant and various veggies.

Russian-style: They call it *shaurma* in Moscow, where they might top it with shredded cabbage and fried potatoes, whereas in St. Petersburg they call it *shaverma* and they stick to tomatoes, cucumber and onion. The sauce could be mayo-ketchup or kefir-mayo concoctions.

Gyros: The Greek Legacy

The *döner kebap* eventually made its way to Greece, where it would become the *gyros*. It was introduced by refugees who had fled Asia Minor (what is now Anatolia, Turkey) between 1915 and 1923. [17]

As the Ottoman Empire was crumbling, it implemented a genocidal policy against its Christian minorities (mainly Greeks, Armenians and Assyrians). It is thought that 1.5 million Armenians and about a million Greeks were killed. The refugees flooded into Greece, increasing the population by a quarter, and bringing their culinary traditions with them, including the *döner kebab*. [18][19]

The *döner* rounds were originally made from ground lamb or beef, but this would change in the early 1970s when the government prohibited the use of ground meat and enforced the use of pork. [20] Some sources say this was due to food safety concerns, others say it was to promote "cheap pork", [21] while others suggest that the Greek dictatorship (1967-1974) wanted to remove Turkish influences, a movement that would continue in the wake of the Turkish invasion of Cyprus in 1974. Anti-Turkish sentiment was expressed in the renaming of things: Turkish coffee became "Greek coffee". [22] The *döner kebap* all but vanished from the streets, and was replaced by the *"gyros"*.

The word "gyros" (pronounced yee-rohs) means "round" or "circle" and is a literal translation of the Turkish word "*döner*". It is unclear exactly when this name change happened, but the *New York Times* was using the word "gyros" as early as 1971. [23]

The Greek Gyros
The Meat:
Slices of pork (or chicken), shaved off the spit.

The Bread:
Thick, fluffy Greek pita bread.

The Toppings:
Tomatoes, onions, French fries. Tzatziki is the condiment of choice in Athens, while Thessalonians sometimes opt for ketchup and mustard.

(Right) Pork gyros cones at Messini Authentic Gyros in Toronto.

The Chicago Story: The American Gyro
"Hydraulic pressure — 60 pounds per square inch — is used to fuse the meat into cylinders, which are stacked on trays and then rolled into a flash freezer, where the temperature is 20 degrees below zero."
- David Segal (The New York Times) [24]

George Apostolou claims to have served the first gyros in the United States, at the Parkview Restaurant in Chicago in 1965. This would pre-date any solid records from New York City, but it is anyone's guess whether they first arrived in New York or Chicago or whether they were convergent.

What we do know is that America's contribution to the history of the döner is its mass production, and that Chicago was ground zero.

Gyro cones are manufactured in factories, with industrialized fillers and preservatives, and shipped all across the United States. A gyro you eat in Arizona will be relatively indistinguishable from one you have in Vermont. The meat is a ground blend of beef and lamb, which indicates that the recipe was brought over to the United States before

American Gyro from Square Boy in Toronto.

Greece switched over to pork. French fries are also omitted, as these were not added to the Greek version until a later decade.

David Segal wrote an in-depth piece about the rise of the American gyro in the *New York Times*, revealing that Gyros Inc. was the first company to mass produce gyro cones in the United States. It was started up in 1973 by an unlikely business duo. Peter Parthenis was an engineer who had a company specializing in rotisseries. One day he was approached by a mysterious man named John Garlic, who wanted to expand his gyro business.

John Garlic was not Greek. He was a big, gregarious Jewish guy, a Cadillac salesman and a former Marine. The story goes that his wife was watching "What's My Line" and there was a Greek restaurateur demonstrating gyro carvery. She immediately called a Greek restaurant in New York, and they told her: "Go to Chicago."

The Garlics managed to get a recipe from a Chicago chef, and they rented a sausage plant in Milwaukee where they made assembly-line gyros, which they sold to universities and festivals.

This is when John Garlic approached Peter Parthenis. Garlic was the "idea man", while Parthenis had the technical know-how. Garlic was a salesman, while Parthenis was a businessman. The pair got the business going, but their clashing styles proved to be an unsustainable partnership.

Segal writes: "There were tensions from the start; Mr. Parthenis says his own buttoned-down style didn't jibe with the unbuttoned Mr. Garlic. According to Ms. Garlic, Mr. Parthenis wanted to run the company on his own. Mr. Parthenis paid the Garlics a modest buyout fee – nobody recalls how much – and the partnership dissolved."

A Greek gyro from Messini Authentic Gyros in Toronto. Unlike the American gyro, it contains pork and French fries.

Peter Parthenis changed the name of the business to Grecian Delight Foods, which is now run by his son, Peter Parthenis, Jr. In a recent interview with *Meat & Poultry*, he spoke enthusiastically about robotic gyro cone slicing technology:

"With ReadyCarved Flame Broiled Off-the-Cone Gyro Slices, it is freezer-to-flattop simplicity." (25)

As for John Garlic, he would go on to buy a restaurant in Milwaukee which had an aquatic side show in a municipal pool, where he kept trained dolphins.

The American Gyro

The Meat: Ground lamb and beef.

The Bread: Greek pita.

The Toppings: Tomato, onion, tzatziki sauce.

In Turkey, *döner* refers only to the meat, and you will have to specify how you want it prepared, in bread or otherwise, whereas in Germany *döner* is synonymous with the sandwich.

The German Legacy

The *döner kebab* entered German consciousness in the 1960s, with an influx of Turkish migrant workers during the *Wirtschaftswunder* (West Germany's post-war economic boom). Xenophobia in the factories, as well as layoffs and other barriers, prompted many Turks to seek self-employment, and the food industry was an available avenue. Turkish immigrants brought their ingredients and recipes to the streets of West Berlin, including the *döner kebab*.

It is widely claimed (mostly by Germans) that before Turkish-German ingenuity, the döner kebab was served on a plate with rice, and nobody had ever thought of serving it as a sandwich. Depending on who you ask, it was Nevzat Salim (1969), Mahmut Aygun (1971), or Kadir Nurman (1972) who "invented" the sandwich. But if you were to consult the Association of Turkish Döner Producers, you would find that official credit has been given to Kadir Nurman. (9)

Nurman opened his snack counter in West Berlin's central train station in 1972, thinking that busy Berliners would like a hand-held take-away lunch. After all, there was certainly a demand for street foods such as currywurst and bratwurst.

Döner fever trickled into uppity neighborhoods in West Berlin and then spread to Frankfurt, Hamburg, Cologne, Munich and various university cities. East Germany finally got a taste in the 1990s, after the fall of the Berlin Wall. Soon the *döner* was out-performing McDonald's, and has been hailed as one of Germany's greatest culinary inventions. (15)

German-style döner kebab.

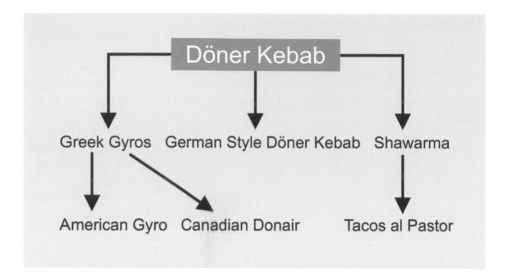

"I'm quite puzzled by all of this," Lebanese writer and chef, Anissa Helou, is quoted in *The Guardian.* "The sandwich has been around forever in the Middle East, so I'm not sure how anyone can claim to have invented it." (9)

Even if we concede that Salim, Aygun or Nurman introduced Europe to the *döner* sandwich, it is difficult to ignore the fact that New Yorkers were already, and quite enthusiastically, eating the gyro.

It would seem that, rather than originating the concept of the sandwich, Germany came up with its own version of the *döner kebab* (and just never bothered to rename it).

German Döner Kebab

The Meat: Beef, veal, lamb, chicken or turkey, either minced or sliced (poultry is always the latter).

The Bread: A wedge of Turkish *pide* bread (thick flatbread), toasted.

The Toppings: A salad of chopped lettuce, cabbage, onions, cucumber and tomatoes. Typical sauces are chili sauce and garlic yogurt.

While Germany is the European heartland of the döner kebab, variations of this sandwich can be found all over Europe. It is a favourite drunk food in the UK, where, in addition to garlic and chili sauce, you might find "burger sauce" (similar to Thousand Island dressing) on your industrialized loaf. The kebab is also popular in Australia, alongside the gyros (also known as "yeeros" or "yiros"). The döner has spread far and wide, taking on new forms and flavours around the world.

Extended Family: Children & Cousins

Sucuk Döner: A rotisserie of *sucuk* sausage rather than *döner* meat.

Stonner Kebab: A Scottish chip shop dish of sausage wrapped in *döner* meat, battered and deep fried. Another popular Scottish dish is the "donner calzone".

Stonner Kebab (Photo: Scoffable on Facebook)

Kapsalon: This is a Dutch dish of French fries baked with shawarma (or doner meat) and gouda cheese in a disposable container, and then topped with shredded lettuce, garlic sauce and sambal (an Indonesian hot sauce). The dish was invented at a shawarma shop called "El Aviva". "Kapsalon" means "hairdressing salon", and is so called because it was the regular order of a hairdresser from a neighbouring salon but caught on among other customers. (26)

Halal Snack Pack: An Australian dish of French fries, doner meat and sauces (chili, barbecue, garlic) in a Styrofoam container.

Halal Snack Pack (Photo: Ghulam Raza)

Tacos Árabes: There was an influx of Christian Arab immigrants in Mexico in the early 20ᵗʰ century, and a Levantine-Mexican creole cuisine started to emerge. Arabic tacos are still a signature dish of Puebla: pork (or lamb, originally) is seasoned with Middle Eastern spices, sliced off the spit into pita-style tortillas and are topped with chipotle salsa. (27)

Tacos Al Pastor: Decades later, the Arabic taco morphed into tacos al pastor, a specialty of Mexico City. Pork is marinated in chillies and spices and stacked onto a spit with pineapple and onion on top.

It is then shaved into soft corn tortillas and topped with cilantro, diced onion and pineapple.

Bánh mỳ Döner Kebab: In Vietnam, pork meat is shaved off the spit and served in a Vietnamese baguette with pickled vegetables and chili sauce.

Bánh mỳ doner kebab stand (Photo: Thanis Lim)

Tacos al Pastor. (Photo credit: Alex Shams, Middle Eastern Eye).

Sandwich Grec: The *gyros* spread to Paris in the 1980s and customers started calling it Le Grec ("The Greek"). Döner meat is shaved into circular bread that is a cross between a pita and a baguette. It is topped with lettuce, sliced tomato and onions, *sauce blanche* (a mayo-yogurt sauce) and served with French fries.

Churrasquinho Grego (Greek Barbecue): A popular street food in São Paulo, Brazil. The meat can be beef, veal, chicken or pork and is shaved into French bread with veggies and vinaigrette. It is commonly served with juice in purple, orange, yellow and red varieties.

3

The Halifax Story

There is a certain mythology surrounding the history of the donair, and it is impossible to recapture the "truth". No one thought to record the milestones, because, well, nobody knew that the donair would travel so many miles and touch so many lives, becoming a cultural icon for a whole nation. Now everyone wants a piece of the pita!

There's a lot of hearsay, nostalgia, downplaying, up-playing and even, I suspect, a bit of a Mandela Effect, whereby the collective memory is inconsistent with public records.

Human beings are notoriously unreliable witnesses. We all process, store and relay information differently. Oral history is laden with hazy memories, emotional bias and opportunistic storytelling. Even written history is full of lazy journalism, archival error, unreliable sources and misleading paper trails.

So, donair history exists in fragments, slivers and vague accounts with large gaps that must be sewn into a story. It is no easy task to weave the tapestry of memories, blog posts, newspaper clippings, promotional materials and public directories. But I have done my best to piece together this stubborn, ill-fitting puzzle, and wrap it up, hot and ready for you.

I first started researching the donair in 2015, and I thought the story was pretty straightforward. I talked to relevant players, family members and aficionados. I read every article on the internet pertaining to the donair.

The story was always more or less the same: a Greek guy named Peter Gamoulakos tried to sell gyros at Velos Pizza in Bedford, Nova Scotia. People didn't like the exotic flavours, so he changed the recipe and people loved it. So, in 1973 he opened King of Donair on Quinpool Road, the first shop to introduce this new food, the "donair", to Canada.

The rest is history!

Or, is it?

One day I was rooting through newspaper clippings in the Halifax Central Library, and I unwittingly opened Pandora's Box. I found an article from 1978, titled: "Donairs find a firm foothold", which had a detailed account of the first five years of the donair.

Extra Sauce

Other examples of Greek-Canadian culinary inventions are:

Hawaiian Pizza - credited to Sam Panopoulos, who immigrated to Canada in 1954. He opened the Satellite Restaurant in Chatham, Ont., which served regular diner fare. But Panopoulos liked to experiment with new foods, and decided to cash in on the growing post-war trend of "Tiki culture" and Cantonese food, which increasingly featured pineapple.

He also started serving pizza, which was a new and exotic food in the late '50s. It was only a matter of time before he dumped a can of pineapple on a pizza, and the rest is history! (31)

Winnipeg Fat Boy – Winnipeg's favourite street food, the Fat Boy, is a hamburger topped with mayo, mustard, onions, lettuce, tomatoes, pickles and a special meat sauce. It is derived from the "Coney Island" hot dog, which was invented by Greek and Macedonian immigrants in the American Midwest in the early 20th century, when they started putting their saltsa kima (meat and tomato sauce) on hot dogs.

In Winnipeg, the recipe has taken hamburger form, and the invention is credited to Gus Scouras, who immigrated to Thunder Bay in 1950, and got a job at his uncle's restaurant, the Coney Island, where he learned the meat sauce recipe. When he moved to Winnipeg, he opened his own restaurant, Junior's, and started serving the chili sauce on his "Lotta Burger". Over time, it became known as the "Fat Boy". (32)

From *The Chronicle Herald*:

"He (Peter Gamoulakos) and one of his brothers opened their first store in Bedford, then called Mr. Doner, where the famous Greek sandwich was introduced… Tremendous success led to expansion: five stores were opened in 1976 with locations on Quinpool Road, Robie Street, Dutch Village Road, Gottingen Street and in Simpson's Mall." (28)

According to the article, the first donair shop was not called King of Donair, but Mr. Doner, and it was located in Bedford (not Quinpool Road). Furthermore, the article suggested that the first store was opened in 1976, not 1973. This changed everything. What else didn't I know?

I decided to see if I could corroborate this information with the public directories and Yellow Pages, sitting in the library with a stack of books taller than my head. I started with 1971 and perused to 1980. There it was: Mr. Doner, in 1976! (For some reason it was "Mr. Doner" in the Public Directories and "Mr. Donair" in the Yellow Pages).

Before 1976, the address on Quinpool Road was listed as a Pizza Delight.

The only King I could find in all of Halifax was a "King of Suits".

The first reference to "donair" I was able to find was a 1974 advertisement for Velos Souvlakia Sunnyside, in Bedford. By 1977, the donair was everywhere I looked. New pizza restaurants were popping up, serving donairs, souvlaki (and tacos, for some reason). Even some of the Italian shops (pizza and pasta houses) were advertising donairs. By 1978, Mr. Donair had been renamed "King of Donairs". I thought, maybe the phone books weren't updated properly. So I checked the Canadian Trademark Database and the Registry of Joint Stock Companies, which both had "King of Donairs" registered in 1977.

People have told me that they remember things differently – that they had a donair on Quinpool Road after they graduated in 1973, or that they drove a certain car that year and remember, beyond a doubt, that it was 1973 when a donair ruined their upholstery.

Even our donair forefathers will insist that donair was being served on Quinpool Road earlier than 1976. And maybe it was. But the corroborative evidence to the contrary is pretty convincing, whereas the human mind is inherently fallible.

To make matters worse, shortly after I discovered the newspaper clipping in the library, it magically disappeared from the folder. If I hadn't taken a photograph, I surely would have thought that I had slipped into a parallel universe!

I reached out to King of Donair to work with me on the timeline, but they have declined to comment.

The following story is my interpretation of events, based on half a decade of research. I have talked to many people, from Yellowknife to Australia. I have dug deep into the dusty archives, and the dark corners of the internet.

Please take it all with a grain of salt and pepper, a sprinkling of oregano, a pinch of cayenne and a good dose of garlic. I have done my best to recover the recipe of past events, from the ingredients available to me at present.

It has been no easy task, but I strongly believe it has value.

Dig in.

Greek History 101

How did this century-old Ottoman food find its way to Halifax, and why the heck does it have a Turkish name? Halifax has sizable Lebanese and Greek communities, but exceedingly few Turks (and we haven't received a large shipment of Germans since the founding of Lunenburg in 1753). So, who was it? Is the donair a funky shawarma, compliments of the Lebanese? Or was it Greek heroes who brought us the yero?

Old picture of Krokees, Greece.

The donair is, in fact, descended from the Greek gyro, but we didn't get the idea from New York or Chicago, which had already adopted the dish by the early '70s. No, the idea was brought over from Greece, not on winged sandals, but on ocean liners, packed with heavy trucks and new beginnings. Greece was experiencing a grand exodus, peaking in the 1960s, as the Greek economy suffered in the post-war years. More than 100,000 Greek immigrants entered Canada between 1946 and 1981. (29)

The plan, for many of the Greeks, was to work in Canada for a few years, building enough wealth to return home and establish a new life. Most, however, did not achieve financial success within the desired time frame, and were also discouraged by the political climate back home. Besides, they were having families and establishing communities. There were Greek churches, schools and festivals, and Greek-Canadians have certainly made their mark on the restaurant scene. (30)

One such family was the Gamoulakos family, and their story is our story.

The Creator: Peter Gamoulakos

Peter Gamoulakos grew up in a small village between two mountains, called Levetsovo (now called Krokees), which is just outside of Sparta. The family lived off the land, but it wasn't exactly an idyllic childhood.

When Peter was quite young, his mother died and Nazi Germany was invading Greece. The Second World War was followed by a Greek Civil War, and his father, who was evidently on the "wrong" side of the conflict, had to go into hiding.

A young Peter Gamoulakos before he immigrated to Canada.

Peter would take his little brother, John, to visit their father when he would sneak into town. They were just boys when they learned that their father had been captured and killed.

More than 1.5 million immigrants came to Canada through Pier 21, on the Halifax waterfront, between 1928 and 1971. It is now home to the Canadian Museum of Immigration. (33)

Peter's coming-of-age was marked by the consequent hardship of a faltering post-war economy. The Gamoulakos children (there were four brothers and four sisters) worked on their grandfather's farm, and found work in Sparta as teenagers, but times were tough. Georgia was the first to emigrate to Canada, and she was followed by Dimitra, Peter, John and George.

Peter Gamoulakos passed away in 1991, but I chatted with his brother, John Kamoulakos, about their first years in Halifax. Peter, who had been living in Canada for several years already, had persuaded John to come over in 1959 and got him a job at the Palace Tea Room.

"Coming to Canada was a slap in the face for me," says John.

"I said to my brother, 'What the hell, did you destroy my life? Coming here to scrub floors for $20 a week?!'"

The cold weather was the other shocker. John told me how he forgot to bundle up one day, and had to run home after work before he froze to death. "My whole face was frozen! They told me my ears and nose almost fell off. All to save 15 cents on bus fare."

After arriving in Canada, Peter worked in a bunch of hotel restaurants in various cities. He wasn't the kind of guy to sit still for very long, but eventually he returned to Halifax, and asked the love of his life, Ester, if she would have him. They married on July 22, 1961.

Family and church were the centre of the Halifax Greek community, and every occasion was a big celebration.

The Gamoulakos family would host big barbecues with wine and lobsters, squeezing as many family members as they could fit into their house.

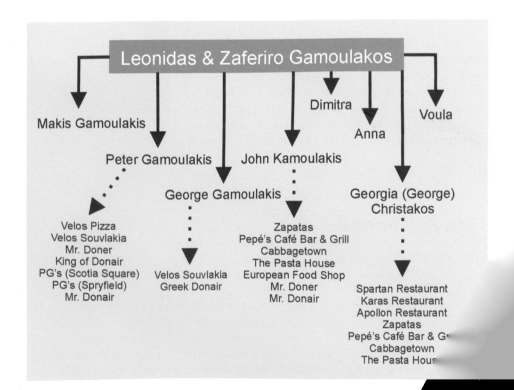

Leonidas & Zaferiro Gamoulakos

Makis Gamoulakis

Peter Gamoulakis

Dimitra

Anna

Voula

John Kamoulakis

George Gamoulakis

Georgia (George) Christakos

Velos Pizza
Velos Souvlakia
Mr. Doner
King of Donair
PG's (Scotia Square)
PG's (Spryfield)
Mr. Donair

Velos Souvlakia
Greek Donair

Zapatas
Pepé's Café Bar & Grill
Cabbagetown
The Pasta House
European Food Shop
Mr. Doner
Mr. Donair

Spartan Restaurant
Karas Restaurant
Apollon Restaurant
Zapatas
Pepé's Café Bar & G·
Cabbagetown
The Pasta Hous·

Peter was also prone to calling up Ester on his way home from work, announcing: "I'm coming over with 10 people!"

Ester would say, "What are you doing, bringing these people here? I'm not prepared!"

But Peter knew that Ester had superpowers. Being the head of a Greek household meant being able to improvise grand hospitality. Ester would defrost the meat and whip up an amazing spread. Their home had an open door, with people always coming and going.

Peter and John also had an old lakeside cabin that they fixed up, and they enjoyed heading out together for hunting and fishing trips. Or they'd have all the family down for ATV rides, boats and fishing. It was here that Peter was said to be in his glory. He would cook for everyone, telling Ester: "In the cabin it's me. I do the work. You relax."

Peter, who had jumped from kitchen to kitchen (like many in the culinary ranks), decided to go into business for himself. He found some success in the pizza business, which had been relatively obscure a decade earlier, but was thriving by the early '70s. His pizzeria, Velos (Greek for "Arrow"), was one of the first in Halifax.

I am not certain exactly when Velos opened, but the earliest record I can find is dated 1972. There were actually two Velos Pizzerias then: one in west-end Halifax (2592 Elm St.), and one in Dartmouth (553 Pleasant St.) near the oil refinery. It would seem that they were both sold off by 1974, and that Peter used the money from the sale to open a new restaurant: Velos Souvlakia Sunnyside in Bedford.

Peter Gamoulakos in 1959.

It is here that donair history begins.

The Early Prototypes

Peter Gamoulakos took the kids on vacation to Greece in 1973, and they returned with gyro fever! Gyros and souvlaki had risen to fast food dominance in Greece in the '60s and '70s, and Peter wanted to introduce Halifax to his favourite Greek street foods.

"...re aren't any hot dogs or hamburgers back home. Donairs, as well as souvlakia, are ...ry street corner in Greece," he told *The Chronicle Herald*. (28)

...noulakos partnered up with Peter Dikaios (his brother-in-law, via Ester), and ..., George, on the new venture: Velos Souvlakia Sunnyside. It was located in downtown Bedford (now a suburb of Halifax), right across the street from the iconic Chickenburger restaurant.

Peter continued to sell the usual pizza and subs, but he got to work right away, setting up a vertical rotisserie and stacking it with meat.

It turns out that making a gyrating meatloaf requires a bit of know-how. Peter's attempts would crumble and fall off the spit, like an ill-conceived sand castle.

Peter Dikaios says that it was George Gamoulakos who "knew a guy" back in Greece, skilled in the art form, and this is who they contacted for instructions. Through a bit of trial and error, Peter Gamoulakos learned how to construct a glorious, spinning loaf. An anonymous commenter on an old blog ("The View from Here") claims to have been the first guinea pig:

"When I worked for Armdale Pizza, my boss took me to his friend's place in Bedford called Velos. It was after closing, and after a round of ouzo, they made a big production out of making me a meal using weird-looking brand new equipment (now familiar to everyone). I had never seen anything like it before. As the Greeks all watched intently, I tentatively (at first) dove into my first-ever donair. I was the first non-Greek to eat a donair in Canada."

Peter Gamoulakos (far left) at Velos Pizzeria, Elm St.

Peter was selling lamb donair and pork souvlakia for 99 cents a pop, and would shave off samples for his customers, but Bedford locals weren't interested. As soon as they heard the word "lamb", they would recoil and resort to the pizza menu.

I tracked down a former employee of Velos Souvlakia, Gus Tectonides, who worked there while attending Mount Saint Vincent University. He says when he started in April of 1974, Peter wasn't exactly raking in the sales.

"Peter was always bemoaning to me that he had sold the Elm Street store," says Gus. "He had been pulling in $500 a week, and that was really good back then!"

Extra Sauce ·-

Gus says that when he left Velos in August of 1974, Peter had started blending beef into the lamb mixture, hoping to make it more approachable. He hadn't dealt with the yogurt yet, which, to shy Maritime palates, had a jolting sour flavour.

The October (1974) Yellow Pages advertises the donair as containing lamb and "cheese sauce". This gives us a glimpse into where we are on the timeline, but it begs more questions than it answers, like, what the heck is "cheese sauce"?

Was Peter trying to make yogurt sound more appealing to the meat 'n potatoes folk, or was something lost in translation?

If Peter was trying to persuade people to eat yogurt by marketing it as cheese, it didn't work. He realized that if he wanted to sell donairs, he would have to figure out what flavours appealed to Canadians. He would have to study them. What brought these people out in droves to the Chickenburger and the Chinese restaurants? Peter likely noted the popularity of sweet and sour dishes, chicken balls and won tons, and figured his customers could be seduced with sweetness.

A 1974 advertisement in the Yellow Pages for Velos Souvlakia

Quinpool Road, 1970. King of Donair would come to inhabit the building beside the Oxford Theatre (Facebook).

He set up sort of a "test lab" in the back of Velos, but by his own account it wasn't exactly Archimedes' bathtub.

"I worked for many years to get the right recipe that would appeal to Canadians," he told *The Chronicle Herald*. (28)

Eventually, he came up with a sweet version of tzatziki sauce that replaced the yogurt with sweetened, curdled milk. It doesn't sound very appetizing when you put it that way, but it is said to have been a resounding success!

According to legend, the newly minted "donair" was such a success that Peter Gamoulakos opened up a whole new shop to specialize in the dish. Apparently, he wasn't getting along with his brother George anyway, so it was time to part ways. Peter Dikaios bought them out and ran Velos for another year or two before selling it (he had coffee to roast, after all). The Gamoulakos brothers would each open donair shops, popularizing the kebab among the late-night bar crowds, and forever imprinting the donair on a generation of students.

Why 'Donair'?

Popular folklore has it that Peter's English-speaking customers asked him what the kebab was called, and he apparently turned around, saw the word "doner" on his imported rotisserie machine, and said, "It is called doner."

This story sounds an awful lot like the old television trope where a character has only a few seconds to come up with an alias, and the camera follows their eyes as they look to objects around the room for ideas ("My name is Door…ahh… Handle. Yes, that's it! Dora Handel."). It also makes it sound like he didn't know what "doner" meant, as if it was a random foreign word that he could anglicize to become a new word with a whole new meaning.

But it wasn't a new word and it wasn't a new meaning. The word "doner" was already used to mean the exact same thing, and Peter was using it well before he developed the sweet sauce (which shoots down my earlier theories that he came up with the word to distinguish it from the gyro).

I actually don't think he saw it as a new invention, but as a Greek food he was introducing to Canada. There is some evidence that the words *doner* and *gyro* were used interchangeably in both Athens and New York in the early '70s, and I suppose this is just another example. Did Peter inadvertently revert to the Turkish name, or was this a stroke of marketing genius?

John Kamoulakos told *The Star* in 2015 that it was locals who morphed the pronunciation. (35) When I asked the Dikaios family, they suggested that Peter Gamoulakos had pronounced "doner" with a French accent. It doesn't seem that anyone remembers it very clearly, and without Peter around, it is possible that it will remain a mystery.

As for the spelling, Halcraft Printers emailed to inform me that it can be attributed to Leo Arkelian, (who bought the printing company in 1949). Apparently he suggested the anglicized spelling when he was contracted by Velos to design their advertising. There it appears, in 1974: "The Donair".

Heavy is the Head that Wears the Crown

"People went there (to King of Donair), from downtown, they would drive or walk, all the ways from downtown to Quinpool Road to get a donair. Lineups were massive. It was extremely busy."
– Leo Gamoulakos, Peter's son

1979 Yellow Pages advertisement for King of Donair.

If you are already familiar with the version of "donair history" oft parroted by the media, you are now expecting me to tell the story of how Peter Gamoulakos opened King of Donair. But that's not what happened next.

The restaurant that he would go on to open was called Mr. Doner and it was actually located on the Bedford Highway. This original location has been lost to obscurity, but there is a listing in the registry of joint stock companies for Velos Souvlakia (1976) that seems to lend evidence for its existence.

After opening the first Mr. Doner in Bedford, Peter opened the iconic shop on Quinpool Road, which, in 1976, was called Mr. Donair.

The Quinpool store was wildly successful, with sales of 600 donairs a day, largely thanks to university students and patrons of the Oxford Theatre.

John Kamoulakos wanted in on the action, and he suggested to Peter that they start a franchise. They approached some businessmen to invest, and formed a company. Then they opened four more locations: Robie Street, Gottingen Street, Dutch Village Road and Simpson's Mall.

Extra Sauce

The building that once housed Greek Donair burned down in 2008, and remained boarded up and vacant until 2016 when the site was revitalized as quintessential summer hotspot Stillwell Beergarden.

"That was a mistake in 1976," John Kamoulakos told me. "We couldn't control it. It was too early. Not that many people knew donair. We spent a lot of money, and the next thing we know we couldn't afford to pay the bills."

Peter decided to buy back two of the locations from the company: Quinpool Road and Dutch Village Road, and he opened a new location in Charlottetown. The other shops were sold off, including the Robie Street branch, which was rebranded to the now iconic Tony's Donair. (28)

Peter also decided to rebrand. By the end of 1977, his three shops were now called "King of Donair".

Peter registered and trademarked the name, but never pushed the issue when other restaurateurs started using the word "donair", mostly because this would mean taking his own family to court. His brother George, notably, had opened Greek Donair (also in 1976), right next door to the Kamoulakos/Christakos restaurant complex on Spring Garden Road. People (especially students) would line up down the street at 2 a.m., waiting for donairs, which were the "exotic bologna" alternative to post-bar egg rolls at The Garden View Restaurant across the street.

With the rebrand to King of Donair in 1977, it would seem that Peter had finally settled on his donair recipe. He told *The Chronicle Herald* that he decided on all beef, with 15 per cent fat. The spice blend was top secret, though, unless you wanted to buy a King of Donair franchise.

According to Gus Tectonides, Peter was selling recipes and equipment for $1,000 when he first started out, but in 1978 Peter appraised the value of a King of Donair franchise at $5,000. (28)

It was a mistake to give away the recipe so early in the game. Many entrepreneurial Greeks started serving the delicacy, and the recipe spread like wildfire. Then the Lebanese started arriving in the mid '70s, fleeing their civil war, and anyone who had

$1,000 could get in on the game. Many Lebanese immigrants got their start in meat shops or pizza shops, and inevitably this all coalesced into donair domination.

It happened quickly. By 1977, virtually every pizza shop in the province was serving the dripping delicacy. That same year, Greco Pizza was established in New Brunswick, with its partner company, Greco Foods Ltd. (now Bonté Foods), mass producing meat cones to supply the growing chain. The secret was out. Peter could hardly sell donair cones to Halifax restaurants anymore because they had figured it out for themselves. He continued to supply all the newcomers with rotisseries and their accessories, and had a local company manufacture rotisserie equipment. Apparently, some of the imported machines had a rust problem, and Peter sold replacement rods of stainless aluminum for $38 a pop. (28)

Of course, he also had three restaurants on his hands, and these would keep him busy all day and night. Being a hands-on kind of guy, he didn't realize the strain that it would have on his life. He started to crave a 9-5 job, with more time for family. So, in 1979 he sold King of Donair and opened a small counter in the Scotia Square mall food court, called PG's, where he made breakfasts and lunches for the downtown office crowd.

Nick & Takis

When Peter Gamoulakos decided to sell King of Donair in 1979, he had two hard-working underlings who were ready to take the crown: Nick Garonis and Takis Mitropoulos.

Nick Garonis was born in 1957 in Papari, Greece (near Tripoli). His family sent him to Canada when he was just 18, to live with his cousin in Halifax, and to make a better life. When he got to Halifax, he quickly found his way into kitchens, and this is where he met Takis. Both young men worked under the table for Peter Gamoulakos, first at Velos, then Mr. Donair.

The original 1983 King of Donair soccer club. They placed 4th in the Canadian Nationals that year. From Nova Scotia Sports Hall of Fame

Nick and Takis had cut their teeth in the donair biz and were ready to take over the kingdom. They also founded the Halifax King of Donair Soccer Team, which was kind of a big deal, winning numerous provincial titles, and most famously, the 2001 Canadian National Soccer Championships. The team was inducted into the Nova Scotia Sports Hall of Fame in 2012.

While working on Quinpool Road, Nick Garonis fell in love with the girl who worked across the street at the Spartan Restaurant, and together they had two sons, Peter and Vasili. Both sons would go on to play varsity soccer for Saint Mary's University, and Vasili even played semi-pro in Greece for a summer. Their athleticism, Peter tells me, was not acquired paternally.

"My father was not an athletic guy," he laughed, when I sat with him in a Halifax coffee shop to learn more about the Garonis legacy.

"My Dad was a social guy. He loved talking to people, bringing things together. He liked when things were happening, when there was movement or buzz. He was the glue that brought people together."

Nick Garonis was most in his element behind the donair counter, where he enjoyed the fast pace and the banter.

By all accounts, he had an insane work ethic and a generous heart. He worked all day, all night, all week, barely getting to see his family.

"I didn't get to see my old man that often until he sold the business," Peter told me.

The King of Donair on Pizza Corner.

"Sometimes I'd wake up because I'd hear his keys getting put on the counter, and that was when we'd have a little bit of time to spend together. I might get up and watch TV for a bit, and I'd fall asleep. It was fun because I wouldn't see him often."

In the late 1980s, Nick and Takis opened a King of Donair on the corner of Blowers and Grafton streets. This intersection would become "Pizza Corner", an iconic Halifax landmark known for its post-bar eats (*read more about Pizza Corner in Chapter 7: The Great Canadian Donair Trail*).

Nick and Takis trademarked the company name and the iconic crown logo in 1987, perhaps with the intention to sell the business. They sold it as a corporate entity in 1989.

Nick Garonis continued his involvement, opening the Lower Sackville branch in 2001. The '90s are kind of a messy decade for donairs and I don't have access to all the fine print. All I can say is that it seems to have been a transitional phase of expansion and acquisition.

A new era was beginning. By 2003, it would seem that Nick had dusted off his hands, and moved on to other pursuits. As for Takis, he drifted off to Montreal where he is rumoured to have briefly opened a donair shop. I'm told that nobody had seen him in 20 years, but when Nick Garonis died in 2015, Takis showed up to the funeral, paid his respects and left town the same day.

Mr. Donair: The Return

While Nick and Takis were running King of Donair, Peter Gamoulakos was getting bored of his day job at PG's. He must have missed the heat of the pizza oven and the glistening donair meat because he decided to open a brand new PG's in Spryfield, this time specializing in pizza and donair.

He also teamed up with his brother, John Kamoulakos, to relaunch the Mr. Donair brand. This time around, they wouldn't be franchising restaurants, but manufacturing donair products. They started out with a facility on Young Street, but decided to downsize the operation to save costs. They renovated the back room of PG's, and moved production there. The front of PG's was a pizza shop, run by Peter and Ester, while the back of the PG's was now Mr. Donair Ltd.

The mass production and distribution of donair products was a whole new game. At first, they'd have a bunch of guys in the back, pounding the meat down on the stainless steel tables and stacking it into cones.

The Donair Kit: just one of many products made by Mr. Donair.

John Kamoulakos, the namesake for Johnny K's Authentic Donairs on Pizza Corner. (Photo: Tim Krochak)

"It was quite a scene," says Nick Giannopoulos, who used to work for Peter Gamoulakos in the late '80s. "Everybody in the back with the stainless steel tables pounding donair meat. We used to pound hundreds of pounds of meat every day."

Eventually Peter and John invested in custom-made machinery, to make production more efficient, and started using a product called "crackermeal" to help bind the meat (whereas before, Peter is said to have used a small amount of bread crumbs).

They sold the donair cones mainly to wholesalers, but they wanted to get into the retail market. A big part of the business was baked donair loaves, which they would slice and vacuum pack to be sold in grocery stores. The development of the "donair kit" hinged on the ability to make the sauce shelf stable.

So, Peter and John invested in pasteurization and sterilization equipment. This was all very expensive, and the brothers knew that in order to get a return on their investment, they would have to market their product nationwide. In order to do that, they needed federal inspection.

But then, in 1991, Peter Gamoulakos died of sudden heart failure. The inventor, culinary heart and creative soul of Mr. Donair – nay, Mr. Donair himself, was gone. John was devastated by the loss of his brother, and found himself alone at the helm of, what he says, was an unprofitable business.

"All those years, I was suffering, never making money out of it," he says.

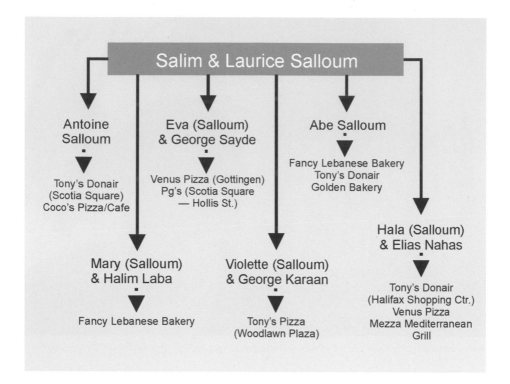

Salim & Laurice Salloum

Antoine Salloum
Tony's Donair (Scotia Square)
Coco's Pizza/Cafe

Eva (Salloum) & George Sayde
Venus Pizza (Gottingen)
Pg's (Scotia Square — Hollis St.)

Abe Salloum
Fancy Lebanese Bakery
Tony's Donair
Golden Bakery

Mary (Salloum) & Halim Laba
Fancy Lebanese Bakery

Violette (Salloum) & George Karaan
Tony's Pizza (Woodlawn Plaza)

Hala (Salloum) & Elias Nahas
Tony's Donair (Halifax Shopping Ctr.)
Venus Pizza
Mezza Mediterranean Grill

In 1995, he decided to outsource production to Antigonish Abattoir (Tony's Meats), which were federally inspected. Tony's Meats took care of the production, trucking and invoicing, which freed up John to focus on the branding and marketing. Tony's paid him a percentage of sales, and it finally started to turn a profit, if not a particularly lucrative one.

"I hired people in Montreal to represent us," he says, "But I was paying a lot of money and not getting any sales."

It didn't look like there was going to be a national breakthrough, so when the contract was up, John decided to sell the business. Tony's Meats bought Mr. Donair in 2005. In more recent years, Leo Gamoulakos, son of Peter, has been championing his father as the true inventor of the donair, and has accused John of over-emphasizing his role in the story.

Leo's claims are not unwarranted. In 2015, a new donair shop opened in downtown Halifax called "Johnny K's" in tribute to John Kamoulakos, who owns the building, and there is a "donair history" written on the interior wall crediting both brothers as co-creators.

But when I spoke to John he was very clear that his brother was the creative genius who came up with the donair. He doesn't have much to say about Leo. The family rift is a touchy subject that the *Toronto Star* delved into a bit in 2015, in which John seemed resigned to indifference.

"If they think I'm the creator of the donair, good luck to them. If they don't think I'm the creator of the donair, good luck to them. Maybe Leo is the creator. Who knows?" (35)

Meanwhile, George Gamoulakos, who played a substantial role in the early history of the donair, had fallen entirely out of the narrative. It would seem he sold Greek Donair by 1978 and moved back to Greece, where, I've been told, he has since passed away.

By 2015, Tony's Meats doubled the business, with a focus on product development and marketing the Mr. Donair brand across Canada. They have stayed true to Peter Gamoulakos's original recipe herbs and spices, making changes only for scale or industry-wide nutrition standards. Mr. Donair has a sizable share of the eastern and western food service markets, but also has a retail line of donair kits, pizzas and sausages. Their most recent contribution to the restaurant world is their Donair Dunkers: deep-fried breaded donair morsels for dunking!

Will the Real Tony Please Stand Up?
"There were a lot of newcomers coming from Lebanon at that time, and we opened the doors."
- Abe Salloum (Tony's Donair)

King of Donair gets a lot of credit for being the "first to introduce donairs in Canada," but Tony's Donair is arguably just as iconic and, as we shall see, more influential. What a lot of people don't know is that Tony's Donair used to be a Mr. Donair. It was one of the stores opened in 1976 when the Gamoulakos brothers incorporated, and it was one of the stores that was sold off when the company disbanded. The Robie Street shop was purchased by a Lebanese entrepreneur, Abe Salloum, who has kept Tony's in the family.

Terry Fox in front of Tony's Donair during his Marathon of Hope, in 1980. From Tony's web site.

Abe Salloum came to Halifax in 1969, after being convinced by his father to move to Canada to further his studies. He had finished his mechanic schooling in Lebanon, and wished to pursue engineering in Halifax.

But everything got turned on its head in 1972 when his father died suddenly. At 24, Abe was now the sole provider for his family. He got a job at the container terminal right away, and he was able to sponsor the rest of his family's passage to Canada. He bought a house for everyone to live in, and opened a grocery on Agricola Street, where everyone could pitch in and work together to pay the bills. (36)

He joined his brother-in-law, Halim Laba, who had a pastry shop, and they started making pita bread for the growing Lebanese community. The Fancy Lebanese Bakery was the first producer of pita bread in Atlantic Canada. Naturally, this is the pita that Peter Gamoulakos had at his disposal when he started making donairs.

Abe Salloum had a good relationship with the Mr. Donair company, so when he nominated another brother-in-law, Tony Helou, to come to Halifax, he was able to get him a job with Peter at the Quinpool store. Tony was working more than 100 hours a week, split between the Lebanese bakery during the day, and Mr. Donair at night.

When Abe caught wind that Mr. Donair was selling off their stores, he thought that a donair shop might be a good addition to the family business. Tony was already well versed in the donair arts, so Abe took out a bank loan in his name and put him in charge. They renamed the restaurant "Tony's" after the three Tonys in the family: there was Tony Helou (commander-in-chief), Tony Salloum (Abe's brother) and Tony Salloum (Abe's son). That's a lot of Tony.

Tony Helou tinkered with the recipe, making the meat spicier. He also added subs to the menu (pizza would come later), and implemented the signature plastic "diaper" that adds an extra layer of protection around the foil-wrapped donair. Tony's brother opened the first expansion attempt, Tony's Donair on Quinpool Road, daring to compete against the immensely popular King of Donair.

It didn't work out. The King was too mighty. The Helou brothers retreated to Ottawa, where they attempted to open a Tony's Donair on Bank Street. When Tony Helou left Halifax, Abe decided it was best to keep Tony's in the family, so he took formal ownership of it.

This all happened between before 1980.

From the beginning, Tony's was an entry point to the work force for many Lebanese immigrants, arriving in Canada during the Lebanese Civil War. It was the training camp for future donair warriors and donair missionaries who would go on to spread the delicacy across Canada.

Because of Tony's:

Greco Pizza

A man named Leander Bourque heard of the late '70s donair boom, and wanted to start his own Moncton-based chain. He reached out to Tony's for education. Schoolmasters Tony Helou and employee Chawki El-Homeira drove to New Brunswick to show him the ropes. In 1977, Bourque founded Greco Donair & Pizza, and its sister company, Greco Foods Limited (the production facility).

So, in a way, Greco Donair is essentially a fast food version of Tony Helou's original recipe.

Greco was purchased by Grinner Food Systems Ltd. in 1981. This was a company established by Bill Hay, a KFC franchisee, who, after trying his first donair, had a vision to grow the industry across Canada. Greco Pizza is now the largest pizza chain in Atlantic Canada and the largest donair chain in, well, I guess you could say, the world. There are more than 100 outlets across Eastern Canada.

Greco Foods Limited morphed into Bonté Foods, and while it no longer owned and operated by Grinners Foods, it is the largest producer of donair products in Canada. Both Greco and Bonté have had a huge impact on the donair, popularizing it around the Maritimes, and introducing it to the national market.

And it all began at Tony's.

Revana Pizza

Employee Chawki El-Homeira graduated from Tony's and opened his own shop, Revana Pizza, which introduced the donair to Dartmouth. When he sold Revana, he sold it to another former employee of Tony's Donair: Jack Toulany

Charles Smart

Chawki El-Homeira not only introduced the donair to Dartmouth (Revana) and New Brunswick (Greco), but he was also instrumental in introducing the city of Edmonton to the donair when he opened Charles Smart in 1982. *(More on that in the next chapter)*

Alexandra's Pizza

Abe Salloum opened a Tony's Donair in the Halifax Shopping Centre in the early '80s (and his brother, Antoine, did the same in the Scotia Square food court). Abe hired a Greek guy named Dimitri Neonakis to run the HSC food stall, and Dimitri would go on to open the Halifax student favourite: Alexandra's Pizza!

Venus Pizza (Mezza Lebanese Kitchen)

In 1990 Abe transferred the Tony's in the Halifax Shopping Centre to his sister, Hala, who was returning to Canada with her husband, Elias (Leo) Nahas, after a stint in Lebanon. After the 10-year contract was up, (early 2000s) they rebranded it to "Venus". This was done in order to align the family businesses under one banner. Elias bought Venus Pizza in the mid-90s and shifted the focus to donairs and Lebanese fare.

Elias Nahas with sons, Peter and Tony. (Mezza Facebook)

Then in 2012 the Nahas family rebranded Venus to Mezza Lebanese Kitchen. *(Read more about Mezza in Chapter 7).*

My Donair

Calgary's first donair shop (as far as anyone seems to know) was My Donair, which was opened in 1983 in the Marlborough Mall. A former Tony's customer wanted to bring his favourite restaurant to his new city. He called up Abe Salloum, who spent a week with him in Calgary, showing him the ropes.

Tony's Donair is like the Johnny Appleseed of the Canadian donair, sowing the fertile landscape with seeds that, over the course of a few decades, have sprouted into a culinary phenomenon.

The Nahas Legacy

The 1970s were the Gamoulakos era.

The 1980s saw the reign of Nick and Takis.

The '90s were the beginning of the Nahas dynasty: brothers Talat (Ted), Elias (Leo) and Bassam (Sam) were laying down the groundwork for what would become the restaurant

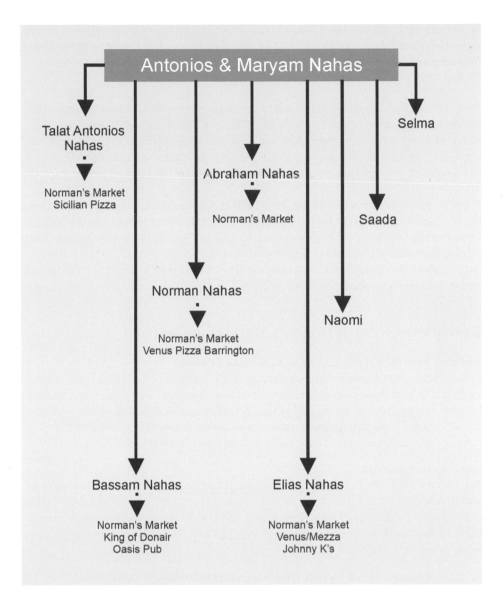

Antonios & Maryam Nahas

Talat Antonios Nahas
↓
Norman's Market
Sicilian Pizza

Abraham Nahas
↓
Norman's Market

Norman Nahas
↓
Norman's Market
Venus Pizza Barrington

Selma

Saada

Naomi

Bassam Nahas
↓
Norman's Market
King of Donair
Oasis Pub

Elias Nahas
↓
Norman's Market
Venus/Mezza
Johnny K's

empires of Sicilian Pizza, Mezza Lebanese Kitchen and King of Donair, respectively. *(More on Sicilian and Mezza in Chapter 7).*

The Nahas family (Antonios and Maryam, with their eight children) boarded the SS Cristoforo in 1967, and sailed to Halifax. Sam Nahas reportedly navigated high school with his Arabic-English dictionary, and graduated from Dalhousie University in 1973. He is a founder of the Canadian Lebanese Chamber of Commerce in Nova Scotia, a property development bigwig, and is known for his work with the Shriners. In 2015, he received an honorary degree from Saint Mary's University. (37)

The guy's kind of a legend.

He bought the Quinpool Road King of Donair in 1989, and over the course of a decade he had become the ruler supreme. By 2006, the franchise had 10 locations in the Maritimes. Sam Nahas owned the trademark, but operated only three of the stores directly. He had a big goal: national expansion.

King of Donair partnered up with a pair of franchise experts, Mark Woodman and Glen Carrigan, and planned to open a whopping 75 King of Donairs across Canada over the course of seven years. That's right: Sam Nahas wanted King of Donair to compete in the big leagues, against the likes of Pizza Hut and A&W! The stores would have bold colours and a retro pizzeria aesthetic, streamlined for efficiency and consistency. (38)

It was an ambitious plan, but the fanfare fizzled and it would seem that the whole thing has been lost to the abyss of forgotten dreams. Sam Nahas turned his attention to his more lucrative work in property development, and in 2009 he handed the reins to his three sons: Andrew, Nick and Norman, who continue to run King of Donair today with youthful energy and creative marketing. They would start laying down the foundation for a new Canadian expansion in 2015.

Examples of King of Donair's Marketing Genius

Anthony Bourdain at the Savour Food & Wine Festival

Perhaps their most famous stunt was driving to the Savour Food & Wine Festival in Wolfville, N.S., to hand deliver a donair to Anthony Bourdain. Norman Nahas hauled his stuff to a pop-up tent set up in a garage. Bourdain had said in an interview with *The Chronicle Herald* that he would love to try a donair but didn't think he would have time. (1) Bourdain is alleged to have said the donair was "marvellous".

Nova Scotia Webcams

Nova Scotia Webcams is a promotional website, launched in 2009, that allows users to watch various parts of Nova Scotia through 24-hour webcams. They now have 70 HD, live-streaming webcams all over Nova Scotia, and are the largest webcam network in Canada. You can watch the waves crash at Peggy's Cove, the historic Lunenburg waterfront, or even the Highland Links golf course.

In 2017, Halifax-based ad agency, Wunder, worked with King of Donair and Nova Scotia Webcams on the "Donair Cam" campaign. A webcam was set up to live stream a donair roasting on the spit. Within just a week, the cam had 47 million impressions from viewers in 159 countries. It was featured by *Vice*, *National Post* and *Buzz Feed*.

Donair Whopper

To raise awareness for International Peace Day 2015, Burger King put out a call for collaboration with their competitors. King of Donair was apparently the only Canadian company to accept the offer to join forces.

For one day only, the two Kings came together at the Quinpool Road location, to serve the "Donair Whopper", a hybrid between a donair and a Whopper for which Burger King sent KOD a shipment of their signature buns.

Nick and Norman Nahas with Anthony Bourdain at the Devour Food Film Festival in Wolfville, NS. (From Twitter @KingOfDonair).

Festive Gestures

King of Donair is known to dye their donair sauce different colours in the spirit of celebrations. They've done green sauce for Saint Patrick's Day, rainbow sauces for Pride, and most recently they've been doing "Gender Reveal Donairs" where the sauce will be either blue or pink when you open the tinfoil.

They have also been a customer of Australian company Pizza Bib, which specializes in decorative pizza boxes that have a slit for your neck so that you can eat from the pizza box without soiling your shirt. The boxes could have anything from a tuxedo, to a leprechaun, to a Trailer Park Boy, depending on the occasion.

For the month of December, King of Donair makes their Holiday Donair, which is a donair with gravy, stuffing and cranberry sauce.

It also celebrates Halifax Burger Week with their Garlieburger: sliced donair meat wedged between slices of garlic fingers. In 2019, they participated in the first Halifax Taco Fest, and this led to a regular "Taco Tuesday" promotion.

Holiday Donair at King of Donair.

Calgary Pop-Up

King of Donair did a pop-up in Calgary's Kensington neighbourhood, in partnership with Meraki Supply Co., East Coast Lifestyle and Alberta Children's Hospital Foundation. It was a raging success, with people lining up for as long as three hours for a taste of Halifax.

DonAir

When King of Donair was creating hype for their Albertan expansion, they put out ads on Facebook and Instagram advertising $7 flights from Edmonton to Halifax. Those who clicked the ads were brought to the flydonair.com website, which looked just like an airline website. Once the user clicked their preference for round-trip or one-way, departure location (Edmonton or Grande Prairie), and number of passengers, a promotional video popped up featuring a flight attendant: "At DonAir, we actually don't fly you anywhere. We don't even have planes. Eating an authentic donair used to mean a trip to Nova Scotia, but with two King of Donair locations now open in Alberta, that's no longer the case." The $7, of course, was the price of a donair.

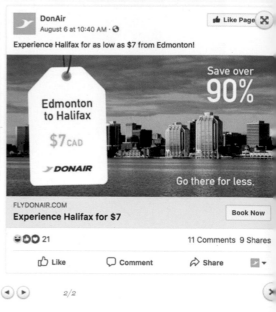

A DonAir ad banner from Facebook.

Make Donairs Great Again

When the company launched its new Grande Prairie store, they decided to create hype by giving away red hats embroidered with the words, "Make Donairs Great Again", fashioned after Donald Trump's popular MAGA hats, to the first 30 customers through the doors. There was lots of online outrage, with people finding the campaign distasteful and offensive. King of Donair responded:

"Just to clarify things with regards to our 'Make Donairs Great Again' hat. We are opening a location in Grande Prairie ... a city that uses tzatziki and lettuce on their donairs. We do not endorse Trump, we're simply bringing Canada's Original Donair to GP." (39)

All publicity is good publicity, right?

In 2018, King of Donair (finally) successfully expanded to western Canada. There are now locations in Edmonton, Grande Prairie and Saskatoon. The donair is making lots of noise with its western awakening, and everyone can finally get a taste of those authentic East Coast flavours!

But wait – any Albertan worth their beef will tell you that they've had donairs in Alberta for a long time now, and they are doing just fine, thank you very much!

So, what's the story with the donair in Alberta?

4

The Edmonton Story

"I would liken donairs in Alberta (and) Nova Scotia to Americans (and) Canadians and hockey. Hockey was born in Canada and most of the best hockey players are Canadian yet the U.S. has a much larger population, therefore they have more potential to exploit the sport. [...] The best donairs come from Halifax yet Alberta has a much larger population."
- Nick Nahas (2)

Know Thyself

Now that the donair had official status in Halifax, King of Donair was ready to franchise nationally. National expansion seems to have been the goal ever since the Nahas family acquired King of Donair. It didn't take off in 2006, but since then we've entered a new era of food fanaticism and national pride, sewn together with social media technologies.

It was a strategic decision to skip over the gyro-and-shawarma-entrenched cities and towns of Ontario. The numbers were out.

In a 2015 promotional handbook, Bonté Foods (the largest distributor of donair meat in Canada) broke down their national donair meat sales into three categories: Atlantic (41%), Alberta/BC (51%) and Ontario (8%). (40) Anyone doing any amount of market research would have seen the flashing arrows pointing to Alberta, where the donair actually has a market and a history.

Legend has it that the donair followed the migratory paths of hungry workers, banished from the Maritimes by poor economies, bringing their work boots and their native cuisine to the cold Alberta barrens. The donair has been around long enough that Alberta has both native donair eaters *and* generations of oil boom transplants from the East. If you drive through Edmonton, you'll see donair shops on every corner. An oversaturated market is better than no market.

King of Donair had done their market research. The next step would be to purge the registries of any similarly named restaurants. There can be only one King. So the process began: cease and desist! Burnaby's Donair King and Calgary's King Donair were two

Nick and Norman Nahas feeding the hungry crowd at the Calgary Pop-up. (Photo: Loren Andrea, Global News).

casualties of the trademark infringement battle. (41) Imagine thinking you were going to get the "official food of Halifax" and instead received one of these Western Canadian Frankendonairs, with pickles and mayonnaise?! The horror…

Friday, March 4, 2016
King of Donair decided to test the market with a pop-up event in Calgary's Kensington neighbourhood. Hundreds of people showed up, waiting for as long as five hours for this taste of the original recipe. The event, (which raised close to $5,000 for the Alberta Children's Hospital Foundation), was so successful that a second pop-up scheduled for the following weekend in Banff was canceled. It would seem that the officials of the Sunshine Village Ski Resort (site of the impending pop-up) were concerned about crowd control. They weren't prepared for the ravenous hoards of the donair-deprived. (42)

Despite the success of the Calgary pop-up, King of Donair decided to open its first shop in Edmonton, and it wouldn't be until 2018. The King had followed on the heels of Calgary's Blowers & Grafton (opened in 2017) and Scotian Style (2016), part of a "new wave" of Halifax-style restaurants infiltrating the province. Like many other street foods and comfort classics, this was propelled by a new generation of tech-savvy, food-obsessed millennials.

With East Coast competition already moving in on Calgary, one might speculate that King of Donair decided instead to set its sights on Edmonton (or, at least, that's where they found a franchisee). But what would a city, already drenched in donairs, think of the "authentic" Halifax donair? There were mixed reviews on Yelp and TripAdvisor:

"Because of only two pita sizes, the medium is a lot of toppings on a teeny, tiny pita. I didn't even see it at first. I tried picking it up but unlike Western donairs that are served in a paper wrap or plastic bag, the aluminium foil barely held it together. It completely fell apart. Most of my bites had no pita but only toppings. … If this is the real thing … I'll stick with my Western Canadian imitation instead."
– Rocky P.

"The pita is warmed on the grill, the donair is then piled on … then gets tossed back on the grill (actually in the same spot as where the donair meat was fried) … when that happens, the sandwich gets super greasy."
- Bert J.

Meanwhile, a recent transplant from Halifax concluded that there wasn't enough grease:

"I think these would be 100% authentic if you let us get a little messy. Give us tons of sauce and grease, that's what the people want."
– Shelbe S.

The main subject of disagreement between Halifax and Edmonton, however, is whether lettuce belongs on a donair. When King of Donair opened on Whyte Avenue, they tried to stay true to their minimalist roots. But when Edmontonians were faced with authoritarian culinary governance, they dug in their heels. Lettuce, or die! Lettuce be free from East Coast tyranny!

King of Donair now offers an "Alberta" donair, with onions, tomatoes, lettuce, cheese and donair sauce.

The Legend of Charles Smart
The Edmonton donair has evolved independently from the Halifax donair, to the point where most Albertans think it is a Lebanese or Turkish dish, adorned with a plethora of sauces and toppings, wrapped up tightly for a fresh and tasty experience. But how did this come to be?

Omar Mouallem wrote a piece for *The Walrus* in 2015 that revealed the origin: the donair was introduced to Edmonton in 1982 by a man named Chawki El-Homeira, or, as he came to be known, "Charles Smart". [43]

Charles Smart has always been this mysterious, elusive character to me. His iconic donair shop was shuttered in 2008, long before I had a chance to visit, and all that remains are nostalgic whispers.

Apparently, his lease was up, and the building, which had been built on the contaminated ground of a former gas station, had to be torn down. It remains a vacant lot of rubble.

I tracked down the phone number for Charles Smart, but my every attempt was greeted by an indecipherable mailbox of static. Being the millennial that I am, I called several times before reluctantly leaving a message, which felt like stuffing a letter into a bottle and tossing it out to sea.

The original Revana Pizza on 90 Portland St. Dartmouth. (Submitted by Jack Toulany).

Weeks went by, until one day my phone rang, and the voice said: "Hello, this is Charles Smart." It was the mythic hero himself! He had just returned from vacation in Phoenix and was kind enough to return my call. I had so many questions.

Charles told me that there were actually a couple of guys doing donairs in Edmonton when he started out, but that they weren't very popular, and that all the meat was shipped from the Maritimes. He was the first guy to make his own donair cones. He made them with Alberta beef, and the way he had learned in Nova Scotia. East meets West.

Charles immigrated to Halifax from Lebanon in 1976, and landed a job at Tony's Donair (back when it was still a Mr. Donair), where he worked for "a Greek guy". He was intrigued by the donair because it reminded him of shawarma; it was both familiar and new to him, symbolic of his new Lebanese-Canadian identity. The next year, he opened his own donair shop across the harbour in Dartmouth: Revana Subs Sandwich (now called Revana Pizza).

In 1978, he sold the shop to Jack Toulany, who moved the shop from 90 Portland St. to 29 Portland, where he still operates. (Charles told me he returned to Dartmouth a few years ago, to revisit his roots, and was surprised to stumble on his old shop a couple of blocks from where he left it).

When Charles sold Revana, he actually left Nova Scotia to visit family in Lebanon. When he returned to Canada, he made a beeline for Fort McMurray, lured, like many Canadians, by the trickling of oil money. His intention from the beginning was to open a donair shop in the boom town.

Alberta was enjoying an oil boom in the 1970s. The price of oil went from $3 US/barrel to $40 US by the end of the decade. Alberta's population grew by a third, and lots of people were getting rich. (44) That is, until it all went bust in the early '80s, shortly after Charles arrived.

His timing was terrible, but he was resilient, and started driving a cab in Edmonton to pay the bills. He saved up his money, and waited for an opportunity. It would come while he was driving his cab; he noticed a sub shop for sale on Whyte Avenue and decided to buy it. (43)

He originally wanted to call his shop Smart Donair: "I was with my lawyer to get my business licence, and I could barely speak English. I told him I want it to be called 'Smart Donair' – as in, good donair (an adjective). The next day I changed my mind – I told him to put my name (Charles) on it. I didn't know exactly what I was doing." The business was registered as Charles Smart Donair.

The next thing he knew, he was getting phone calls from the Smart family in British Columbia, inviting him to family reunions! "That's how I found out it was a last name," he laughed.

Charles Smart Donair. From Wikimapia.org

Chawki El-Homeira would thenceforth be known as Charles Smart.

The place he bought was a hamburger and sub shop, but he set up his first donair cone in 1982. It was football sized, weighing five to six pounds, and he would slice off samples to give to his customers when they came in for a sub or a burger.

He says the reaction was instantaneous. People returned the next day to try a donair, and would tell their friends, spreading the good word of Charles Smart.

One side of his building was the restaurant, but the other side was a meat facility where Charles made donair cones to sell to Lebanese restaurateurs around the city.

By the mid '80s, he was federally inspected, and started shipping cones to B.C. and Manitoba. He had a large freezer in his front window, and you could see the frozen meat cones on display.

He noticed that window gazers were intrigued by the cones, so he decided to do a publicity stunt: he made a giant donair cone that, according to Roadside America, was six feet tall and 567 pounds!

"I wanted something to attract people to the donair," he told me. "When I started, nobody had any idea of donair in the city."

It worked. People started showing up with cameras, and soon all the newspapers were covering it.

Suddenly, everybody in Edmonton knew about donair.

Charles said he originally meant to expand the menu to include pizza, like the shops back in Halifax, but the donair took off right away and he never had time. His hands were happily full.

By the 1990s, the donair was Edmonton's favourite street food. Charles Smart sold donair meat to a lot of the local restaurants, but the Lebanese restaurant community was not without its drama.

One of Charles's customers, Sam Tawachi, figured out how to make the meat cones, and started competing. It is said that he would badmouth Charles Smart to his whole-sale customers, that he was sneaking pork into his meat blend. (43) The real problem was that Charles came from Halifax, where the Lebanese community is predominantly Christian. His donair meat was not halal.

Despite community bickering, the loyal, hungry, tipsy Whyte Avenue customers kept on coming through his doors, including, he says, some of the Edmonton Oilers. Charles Smart Donair had risen to iconic status; it was the template for all Edmonton donairs, and the standard by which they would all be judged.

"The key to a Charles Smart donair is the way the sauce, meat juices, and spices combine to form this kind of slurry that is so intoxicating you can't help but shovel it into your mouth with your bare hands like an animal," according to Reddit user BlockParent. "By the end your hands and face are covered in sauce, and the one tiny little napkin they gave you has been completely destroyed."

Sam Tawachi, the alleged "saboteur", would end up opening the behemoth Athena Donair Distributors in 1995, which now supplies the majority of Edmonton's donair shops. (43)

Fun Fact: Edmonton is home to the oldest Muslim community in Canada, and the very first mosque built in Canada was the Al Rashid Mosque, constructed in 1938. (45)

Both Charles and Sam, despite their differences, have had a lasting impact on the Edmonton donair, and made a good life for themselves and their families.

Charles was able to retire comfortably, but he told his children: "I was first generation, I worked very hard. I had to work 20 hours a day. You are second generation, you've been educated. You shouldn't do this work."

He had six children, who continue to love donairs, and everyone in the family still makes them at home, or for church fundraisers.

There was something I just had to know: why lettuce, I asked him?

He told me that 98 per cent of people would order their donair the Halifax way, but as people associated the shop with subs, and lettuce is good on a sub, they would ask for it on their donairs.

"Some people would ask for French fries," he said. "We added cheese on it later on, when people started asking."

But does lettuce *belong* on a donair, I asked him?

"Lettuce does not belong, no."

The Nation Network's Jay, Cam, and Karim at a Burger Baron. From The Nation Network: Nation Donair Tour – Burger Baron (YouTube).

The Oregano Trail

Charles Smart may have introduced the donair to Edmonton, but it was the Burger Baron that is largely responsible for spreading the donair far and wide.

The guys from The Nation Network, an Edmonton-based NHL blog and fan site, reviewed more than 20 donair shops on a YouTube series they called "Nation Donair Tour".

"Sitting on the back of a pickup truck by a Burger Baron, (an iconic hamburger restaurant in Western Canada) critiquing the donairs, they speculated that Burger Baron was the first to bring donairs to Edmonton: "They came across the country on a wagon and a horse, with the donair, with the meat on the thing, and they were the first ones."

It was the Oregon Trail of Albertan donairs, they joked.

Omar Mouallem's father, Ahmed, was one of these pioneers. He was the first to introduce the donair to High Prairie, Alberta, when he opened a Burger Baron there in 1987, and Omar has echoed the notion that Burger Barons played a large role in the spread of donairs across Alberta.

Back in the day, there were only two guarantees you would have in small-town Alberta: there'd be a Chinese restaurant, and a Burger Baron.

Burger Baron was the first drive-thru chain in Western Canada, founded in 1957. But the original franchise went bankrupt when the big American chains entered the market, and now every Burger Baron is independently owned." (46)

At some point, all the Barons started selling donairs, but the donairs were secondary to hamburgers, and many of the Burger Barons bought frozen, sliced donair meat (and pre-made sauce) from the big wholesalers.

"My father's donairs weren't perfect," Omar Mouallem wrote in *Swerve*.

"He had no compunction about using frozen pre-cooked slices and slathering the meat with an unconventional yogurt sauce more appropriate for Greek food. But he was anal retentive about using quality pita from a trusted Lebanese baker, sometimes driving to 'the city' to get it fresh." (46)

I asked Omar why Edmontonions put lettuce on their donairs.

"They (the Lebanese restaurateurs) wouldn't think not to add vegetables because, if you've had a shawarma, it's just as much about the vegetables as it is about the meat. When they were selling the donair, they treated it like a shawarma. But they also understood that pickled veggies aren't going to work with this sweet sauce. So they used burger toppings, because they were already selling burgers. The sliced tomato, the shredded lettuce and diced onion, are already things you would have if you were selling burgers. They'd put the meat on the grill with the steak weight on it. It was more like throwing burger patties on the grill."

A Lebanese hamburger.

Anatomy of an Edmonton Donair

"I think it's ridiculous that the hard-line Halifax donair groupies insist their version is better. The instant you label something inauthentic and therefore worse due to the addition of a topping or experimentation, you strangle its growth. Food is about nourishment and community, not a reason to build an exclusive traditionalist club that demands food to never change and always stay the same."
– Dan (Edmonton donair enthusiast)

The Edmonton donair features the same spicy spitted beef as the Halifax donair, but it is markedly different, and just as people fixate on the sweet sauce as the defining characteristic of the Halifax donair, people seem to fixate on the lettuce when it comes to Edmonton.

But there is so much more to each style. The Edmonton donair, I would argue, is best defined by its tight wrapmanship.

To eat it, you unwrap the foil, (which is a robust type of foil, lined with paper), and hold the donair by the plastic bag at the bottom.

Watching the guys on Nation Network casually eating their donairs with one hand, while fully able to gesture with their other, betrays the stylistic difference between east and west.

The Edmonton donair is a fist food, whereas Haligonians are largely resigned to eating their donairs off the table (or floor – don't judge).

The default Edmonton donair is cheese, lettuce, onions, tomatoes and sweet sauce in a steamed pita.

Edmonton-style Donair from Queen Donair.

The Meat: The largest supplier of meat is Athena Donair Distributors, but there are also Aladdin and other competitors. There are also chicken donairs, made from a shawarma-style roast.

The Sauce: In Edmonton they call it "sweet sauce", to distinguish it from other possible donair sauces, most notably sour cream, yogurt, or mayonnaise-based sauces. Some reports say the sauce is a little less sweet than the Halifax version.

The Pita: The Edmonton pita is cleanly steamed, for a soft, warm, supportive grip. This is in stark contrast to the greasy, grilled Halifax pitas that have more moisture and chew. Jay Downton ("The Squire" on *The Nation Network*) compared the Halifax pita to a yoga mat.

The Cheese: Say what you want about the sauce and pita, but Edmonton has mastered the art of the "Cheese Donair".

The Toppings: The No. 1 thing that differentiates an Edmonton donair from a Halifax donair is the lettuce. But many shops will have a toppings bar full of other possible additions.

The farther you get from Edmonton, the more the identity of the donair weakens. Fort McMurray definitely has a donair scene, but a lot of shops there allegedly put mayonnaise in their donair sauce.

And if you head south, you enter shawarma country. Edmontonians complain about the "shawarma donairs" of Calgary, with their lack of meat and loose wrap jobs. I've even caught desperate transplants in Vancouver inquiring of online forums: "Where can I get a good Halifax-style donair, like the ones in Edmonton?"

Charles Smart brought his Nova Scotia recipe, but the restaurateurs that would follow were not familiar with the food.

He supplied them with the meat, but there was no tradition of how to prepare the wrap, so the recipe was interpreted and adapted in its own social and cultural context.

It had its own evolution in Edmonton, parallel to Halifax, and a distinctive style emerged in the "second city". The early adopters were all Lebanese, so everyone assumed it was a Lebanese food, and the Lebanese shop owners happily indulged that mythology. The shawarma was the existing template, but a more subdued, less colourful garden was applied.

In 2016, I travelled to Edmonton to study this "Prairie Donair" and I was surprised by the resemblance to the Halifax style. The essential conditions were met: spicy ground beef wrapped in a warm pita with sweet milk-based sauce. Hold the lettuce. No problem.

But when I furthered my study in Calgary, it was like the donair had played the "telephone game" and the original meaning was lost in transmission.

The Calgary Situation

"Arabs call them 'shawarma', the Greeks refer to theirs as 'gyro', for the Turks they're 'doner kebab', but, to most Canadians, they are simply called 'donairs'. No matter what they're named, however, they all mean just one thing: an enticing dish made from a heady mixture of spiced meats, tasty veggies and tangy sauce generously jammed into a pita."
– from Basha Donair's website

The above quote pretty much sums up the perception of the donair in most of Western Canada. The word "donair" is just a Canadian word for a generic dish of meat wrapped in pita bread. It is presumed to be a Turkish dish (based on spelling) or an Arabic dish (based on vendors), and that's essentially what it is: a shawarma doner.

I was surprised to learn that the donair has been in Calgary since the early '80s. Bassil Sleiman, of Uncle Moe's Donair, tells me that the first donair shop in Calgary was My Donair, which originally opened in the Marlborough Mall in 1983. (You'll remember that Abe Salloum of Tony's Donair in Halifax visited Calgary for a week to teach one of his old customers how to run a donair shop.) More people got involved and started opening up their own My Donair outlets, some of which are still My Donair, while others have rebranded.

too many variables, from the size and shape of the donair cone, to the temperature and distance of the heat source, to the "trimming accuracy" of the employee serving it.

The working group came up with a list of recommendations based on their findings. Many of them were related to the manufacture of donair cones, but several of the recommendations would have an effect on the way restaurants do business. In particular, they recommended smaller cone sizes, better cooling and storage procedures, and a secondary cooking step.

Recommendation #5: Secondary Cooking Step
Portions sliced from a donair cone should undergo a secondary cooking step designed to achieve a temperature of 71°C (160°F) in the case of beef, lamb, and pork containing products or 74°C (165° F) in the case of chicken containing products.

This may be the most pivotal of the mandates, because it essentially changed the way that donairs are prepared. Purveyors used to serve the meat directly from the donair cone. Now it is standard practice to grill the meat on the flattop before serving it. *The Globe and Mail* reported in 2008 that some shop owners claimed the slice-and-serve technique was "integral to the dish."

"But a visit last night to Pizza Corner (in Halifax) showed that the double-cooking method is variably applied. One restaurant did it whichever way the customer wanted, and staff at another said there was no need to cook the meat a second time. Only at one did the clerk say it was crucial to cook the meat again after slicing it off the spit." (50)

Omar Mouallem says the Edmonton outbreak had less to do with any inherent danger, and more to do with the Oilers having a good season. They made it to the Stanley Cup playoffs in 2006. Donairs were selling faster than the vendors could cook the meat.

"You couldn't drive down Whyte Avenue," he told me.

"There were all these people coming out of the arena, and out of sports bars and dorm rooms. It was an unprecedented demand, which makes me reconsider the necessity of the donair working group."

Omar suggests that this might have been a bureaucratic response to an unprecedented thing.

So, what about the Calgary incidents? It turns out that the outbreak was linked to a major beef distributor that also supplied the Wendy's chain. Yet there wasn't a "federal-provincial-territorial **hamburger** working group". Is this the same sort of "doner discrimination" as was decried in Germany when the EU threatened to ban phosphates in doner meat, while exempting traditional sausages? Or how "Chinese restaurant syndrome" doesn't affect people when they eat Doritos?

While we may have Alberta to thank for our twice-cooked donair meat (a blessing or a curse, depending on who you ask), a 2004 article in *The Chronicle Herald*, "N.S. Donairs: They induce babies, upset tummies and make us homesick" is evidence that Nova Scotians were well aware of the donair's powers, despite never having any reported cases of food poisoning.

The Ballad of East and West

"All I want on a daily basis is a good old Nova Scotia donair. Out here they have 'donairs', but they have lettuce and tzatziki sauce on it, if you're lucky. Otherwise it's ranch dressing. And the meat… is so bland… it's like eating bologna. It makes my tongue cry." Melissa Richards wrote from Lethbridge to The Chronicle Herald *in 2004.* (51)

Why are Maritimers so averse to Albertan donairs, and why are Albertans not usually impressed when we introduce them to Halifax donairs?

I consulted radio personality Yukon Jack, who, I was told on good authority, was an expert on donairs.

I asked him: "What would you say is the difference (besides lettuce) between an Edmonton donair and a Halifax donair?"

His response: "The main ingredient … nostalgia."

An example of a Calgary "shawarma-style" donair that, in this author's opinion, is pretty sad looking.

Donair meat at A-1 Pizza in Liverpool. (Photo by Vernon Oickle)

5

Anatomy of a Donair

"Just break it down: it's bread, meat, sauce, onions, tomatoes - that's it. That's technically a donair if you break it down under a microscope. But I feel like it's the people who make it. They take it from beyond those five ingredients and they turn it into something special. It's like your mom's soup or whatever... Someone else could make that soup, but it just won't be the same. There's something that just transcends the confines of the donair."
- Neil MacFarlane (donair enthusiast).

The Meat

"You have to have a good meat. That's the beginning and that's the end. Forget what you're cooking if you don't have good meat," Jaco Khoury told me over the phone. A self-described "donair warrior", with a legacy that stretches from from Beaver Bank, N.S., to Saint John, N.B., Jaco was pleased to talk about his impromptu career choice.

Jaco was the face of Shubie Pizza from 1995 to 2008. An electrical engineer by trade, he found himself thrust into the pizza world when he immigrated to Canada, and he decided to make the best of it by opening his own shop and making a name for his pizza and donairs.

"There were 10 guys from Elmsdale to Truro," he told me. "We all had pizza shops, but not franchises – we each had our own recipe, all competing."

Back in those days, most pizza shops were still making their own donair meat, and Jaco came to the realization that the secret to a good donair is the quality of the meat. "As small businesses, we would buy meat from IGA or Sobeys, and it depends ... if he cuts you good meat you get a good donair. Otherwise your meat sucks for a week and you can do nothing about it!"

So Jaco started asking around, looking for a superior source of meat. He decided to reach out to his pepperoni guy, who, to his surprise, admitted that he imported beef from New Zealand. It came frozen, in 60-pound boxes, but it was "beautiful meat".

So Jaco ordered a couple of boxes of 70 per cent lean. When the meat arrived, it wasn't pre-ground. Jaco now had 120 pounds of meat, and there was no butcher in his village to grind it. He had to shop around for a commercial grinder, finding one for $300.

Then he got to work, grinding, mixing, freezing, thawing and spicing it just the way he liked. People started to notice, and soon he was getting 200 to 300 pounds of meat at a time.

"I was selling a thousand pounds of donair a week and I couldn't keep up," he said. "It was a nightmare!"

The glory days of Shubie Pizza lasted only a few years before the whole process wore him out. Jaco's doctor told him he needed cortisone in his elbows and shoulders, which were busted from all the grinding and mixing. But he remembers those days fondly.

"You want to eat a donair that will blow your head away? I miss that donair."

After a brief retirement, Jaco opened up a new shop in Saint John.

His first supplier allegedly sold him shoddy donair meat, and the dispute ended up in court.

Jaco told the judge that there was excess fat melting under the broiler and causing the adhesion of the meat to fail. After being ordered to split the costs, Jaco decided to take his business elsewhere. (52)

He says Bonté Foods was willing to develop a recipe with him when they saw how much volume he was pushing. Jaco still stakes his reputation on the quality of his meat, which, he says, is made exactly to his specifications.

The Industrial Revolution

You can't just slap a loaf of meat on a spit and spin it around a flame. It is a whole process that requires labour, time, skill and the right materials.

"You have to use so much lean and so much fat to get the right texture," says John Kamoulakos.

"Too much lean, it tastes like leather. Too much fat and it falls all over the place."

His brother Peter used a ratio of 85 per cent lean to 15 per cent fat, but the practice today often involves a lot more fat and breadcrumbs, especially as the price of beef has steadily risen. (53)

Then there is the arduous stacking process.

Nick Giannopoulos, who used to work for Peter Gamoulakos in the late '80s, tells me that they used to stack the raw meat with rings of cooked donair meat, which would help structure the heavy, drooping meat pile.

"This is why you couldn't serve the inner core," another former employee told me.

"It would be too brittle and dry."

Dimitri Neonakis also remembers this process. "They used to fall off and crack, so we used to give them a bit of a base in the middle of the stick."

"But that wasn't a very common practice," he told me.

As the cone was stacked, blobs of meat would hang down in the physique of a sumo wrestler, and the excess rolls would be sliced off. The pile of meat would be cut into a cone shape, and smoothed out with a spatula that you'd usually find at a hardware store. Finally, the cone would be patted down with wetted hands and popped in the freezer.

There are different ways of doing it, of course. Many practitioners have learned the art by trial and error, and they guard their techniques with utmost secrecy.

In the '70s and '80s, it was common for each shop to have its own recipes and techniques, but there was a gradual shift in the '90s to outsourcing donair cones to specialists.

A specialized producer could make donair cones with more efficiency and consistency, and by the turn of the millennium, the majority of Halifax-area pizza shops were getting their donair meat from a handful of suppliers. There was Mr. Donair, of course, and there was Bailey's Meats, a meat-shop-turned-donair-wholesaler that at one time

A-1 Pizza in Liverpool, N.S. (Photo: Vernon Oickle)

Factory workers packaging donair sausages at Mr. Donair. (From Mr. Donair)

serviced a substantial amount of donair shops in Nova Scotia with cones (but has since scaled back to a handful of loyal customers).

But if you eat a donair in Halifax today, chances are the meat came from Leo's Donair (informally referred to as "Toulany's"). Leo Toulany supplies the majority of donair meat to Halifax-area pizza shops, from his provincially inspected plant, with each restaurant's secret spice blend on file.

Leo Toulany immigrated to Canada in 1976, just as the donair was beginning to take off, and like many in the Toulany family, he was trained as a butcher.

Leo's first meat shop was called Toulany's Meats, which was located at 5576 North St. in Halifax. A few years later, he moved the shop to Herring Cove Road, and was there for a decade or so, selling pizza and supplying local restaurants with meat, fish, cheese and cold cuts. In 1987, he opened Timberlea Discount, which was sort of a convenience grocery with video rentals and fresh meat. By 1994, he had added donair cones to his butchery repertoire.

When people hear "Toulany" they usually think of Leo's cousin, Bash Toulany, who was a major player in the donair game throughout the 1980s to the 2000s. He famously transitioned his Duffus Street meat market into Halifax's favourite donair shop, and helped popularize the dish by selling frozen donair meat through Loblaw and Sobeys.

To make matters even more confusing, another cousin, Habil Toulany, operates Billy Stick Foods, a donair facility in Lake Echo, known for their signature "Billy Sticks" (donair Pogos).

Bash retired in 2008, but Leo had his eyes on expansion. In 2010 he closed the Timberlea grocery and increased factory production of donair cones. In addition to being a wholesale distributor, Leo's now has a retail shop where customers can buy donair products.

But while Leo's Donair dominates the Halifax market, his donair meat is not federally inspected, so you won't find it anywhere else.

"The best meat is Leo's meat," says Josh Robinson, of Alberta's Blowers & Grafton. "It's got the perfect amount of fat and spice."

He's waiting patiently, hoping one day he'll be able to serve Toulany's to his Albertan clientele.

Alberta has had its own trajectory of donair market domination, pioneered by Charles Smart, who had his federally inspected plant by the mid-'80s. He was followed by Global Donair, Athena and Aladdin, who now compete in the western market alongside the federally inspected Bonté Foods (Dieppe, N.B.) and Mr. Donair (Antigonish, N.S.).

These palaces of stainless steel transform ground beef into an orangey paste, and squeeze it into moulds using hydraulic pressure or vacuum.

Leo's Meats now has a retail store in Timberlea, Nova Scotia, where you can buy donair products. (Photo: Kira Noble).

Each company has its own formula, consisting of emulsifiers, preservatives, flavour enhancers and industrial fillers. Athena's product contains beef, toasted wheat crumbs, spices, salt, monosodium glutamate, modified cornstarch, and sodium phosphate, for example, but if you want to pinch a few pennies you can opt for less premium versions, bursting with soy and starch. (54) It may not *sound* appetizing, but most of the people who are fearful of this "mystery meat" will readily scarf down a feed of chicken nuggets.

The alternative, of course, is to make your own.

Recipe

GLEN PETITPAS'S DONAIR RECIPE
(ADAPTED FROM DEREK STAPLETON)

Ingredients

3 POUNDS LEAN HAMBURGER (TRIPLE GROUND*)

3/4 CUP BREAD CRUMBS

2 TSP PEPPER

1-2 TSP CAYENNE RED PEPPER
(DEPENDING ON YOUR TASTE)

1 1/2 TSP OREGANO

3 TSP PAPRIKA

2 TSP ONION POWDER

1 TSP GARLIC POWDER

1/2 TSP SALT

Directions

COMBINE ALL INGREDIENTS IN A LARGE BOWL. KNEAD FOR 20 MINUTES. SHAPE INTO TWO TIGHTLY FORMED LOAVES. BAKE ON BROILER PAN FOR 2 TO 2 1/2 HOURS AT 300 DEGREES FAHRENHEIT. COOL LOAVES AND SLICE INTO THICK SLABS. MEAT CAN BE FROZEN FOR FUTURE USE. IF (LIKE ME) YOU ARE NOT FORTUNATE ENOUGH TO OWN YOUR OWN ROTARY-STICK-COOKER THING LIKE THE ONES IN THE GOOD SHOPS, YOU MAY FIND THAT THE INNER PARTS OF THE LOAF ARE NOT BROWNED ENOUGH. THIS CAN BE REMEDIED BY RE-HEATING THE MEAT IN A FRYING PAN. THIS BROWNS IT NICELY AND GIVES IT THAT SLIGHTLY CHEWIER TEXTURE.

*TRY TO GET YOUR BUTCHER TO RUN THE MEAT THROUGH THE GRINDER A FEW TIMES. A FOOD PROCESSOR WILL DO THE TRICK ALSO.

The Major Players

'The Original' Mr. Donair

Mr. Donair was the first facility dedicated to the mass production of donair meat in Nova Scotia. It was founded in 1985 by Peter Gamoulakos himself, who brought his brother John Kamoulakos on as VP.

Tony's Meats, in Antigonish, N.S., acquired Mr. Donair in 2005. Today, "The Original" Mr. Donair TM is a well-known brand for both household and commercial products. They supply more than 1,000 restaurants across Canada with donair meat and sauce.

Bonté Foods

Greco Donair, and its sister company, Greco Donair Foods (now Bonté Foods), were both opened in 1977; the former was a restaurant franchise and the latter was a processing plant to support the fledgling chain. This was New Brunswick's first foray into the donair, and a driving force in popularizing it around the Maritimes. In 1981, Bill Hay was looking for a storage and distribution centre for his KFC franchising company when he approached the Greco facility. He tried his first donair, and ending up buying the company. (55) Bonté Foods was the first to expand the donair into Western Canada, and continues to be a national leader today. Within the last decade they have converted to a gluten-free facility and have acquired halal certification for all of their donair and gyro cones.

Athena

In 1990, Sam Tawachi produced donair cones for his restaurant, and also distributed them throughout Alberta. In 1995, he left the restaurant business, and Athena Donair became a federally inspected processing plant. It is now one of the largest donair distributors in Canada. In 2004, he moved to a 17,000 square-foot state-of-the-art facility. (54)

The Sauce

"If a salted caramel dark chocolate brownie is a finely tuned high-octane engine for the tastes, donair sauce is rubbing two sticks together over a pile of oily rags. Brutal in its simplicity, but also in its intensity."
– Denton Froese (my friend, the chemist)

The great Canadian donair can be dressed with any number of sauces, usually with some sort of white creamy base, whether it be yogurt, sour cream, mayonnaise or condensed milk. But the most characteristic sauce, especially for a Halifax-style donair, is the so-called "sweet sauce".

Donair sauce squirted onto a donair from a squeeze bottle at Tony's Donair (Photo: Dagley Media).

In the Maritimes, it is simply called "donair sauce" because it is the only sauce that is supposed to go on a donair. It is not exclusive to donairs (it is also used as a dipping sauce for pizza and garlic fingers), but to put any other type of sauce on a donair is a blasphemy particular to the East Coast. If you put tzatziki sauce on a donair there is a chorus of Haligonians, somewhere, right now, at the ready, to proclaim: "That's not a donair!"

While the sweet sauce is the most obvious thing that separates a Halifax donair from a gyro, simply adding donair sauce to a gyro doesn't make it a donair, and by the same logic, putting tzatziki sauce on a donair doesn't render it a gyro. I would argue that too much emphasis is placed on the sauce, when there are more important things to worry about, like cold pita bread and pickled turnip!

Those who dislike donair sauce, (and there are many, even in the Maritimes), claim to dislike it for its sweetness. This is delightfully ironic, because back in the '70s Peter Gamoulakos had to sweeten the sauce because people didn't like the (now trendy) yogurt.

You have to realize that in the early '70s, yogurt was still a relatively new product in North America. It was popular with a few fringe health nuts early in the 20th century, like John Harvey Kellogg, who prescribed, um, yogurt enemas, (56) and it started to gain some traction as a health food in the 1950s, but Americans didn't like the sour taste. Someone eventually realized that Americans will eat anything if there's enough sugar in it, so in 1966 fruit-on-the-bottom was invented and the rest is history! (57)

Sonia Jones's 1987 book *It All Began with Daisy* details her journey from New York City to buying a cow in Nova Scotia, and haphazardly starting up Peninsula Farms Yogurt (1975-2000).

"It was an uphill battle all the way," she writes, "for many people saw yogurt as a rather exotic food compared to their usual fare of codfish and potatoes." (58)

This sentiment is echoed by Mike Nico-letopoulos, a longtime volunteer at the Halifax Greek Festival, and who grew up making donairs at his father's restaurant, Island Greek, which was the first to serve donairs in Cape Breton.

Thick donair sauce ladled on a donair at A-1 Pizza in Liverpool, N.S. (Photo: Vernon Oickle)

"We used to get big buckets of feta, and Cape Bretoners used to make fun of us for the smell. In those years, anything that was different was tough for people."

Original recipe donair sauce with a bit of separation.

Just as yogurt companies had to sweeten their product to make it palatable to Americans, Peter Gamoulakos came to the same realization about his gyro sauce.

The original recipe was, more or less, equal parts evaporated milk and sugar, flavoured with garlic and parsley, and thickened with vinegar. It's sort of like a sweet version of tzatziki sauce, except the premise of the sauce is evaporated milk curdled, as it were, with vinegar.

Milk is full of free-floating protein molecules, but when you change the pH balance, by adding vinegar, the molecules attract one another and form clumps. There is an unstable period, teetering between order and chaos, where you might find yourself with a beautiful, thick donair sauce, or, sitting on your tuffet with a runny mess. She's an unforgiving mistress, as anyone knows who has tried to learn her magic. One wrong move and you'll break the sauce. Look at it the wrong way, and it will self-destruct, unraveling proteins and hostile acids resisting this alchemical assimilation.

Whipped donair sauce from Joey's Pizza in Sackville, N.B.

What's puzzling is that you could just as easily end up with a whipped cream. (This is what evidently happened at Liverpool Pizzeria on Nova Scotia's South Shore, and they decided to just roll with it).

Traditional donair sauce is medium thick and the flavour should not be jarringly acidic or garlicky, nor should it be dessert-like. It is an impossible choir of flavours and textures that shouldn't harmonize, but they do. There is nothing quite like it. Here's how you do it:

Recipe — ORIGINAL DONAIR SAUCE RECIPE

Ingredients

2/3 CUP EVAPORATED MILK

2/3 CUP SUGAR

1/4 CUP WHITE VINEGAR

1/2 TSP GARLIC POWDER

Directions

MIX TOGETHER MILK, GARLIC POWDER AND SUGAR.

STIR UNTIL SUGAR IS DISSOLVED.

POUR IN VINEGAR, AND STIR A FEW TIMES.

REFRIGERATE FOR SEVERAL HOURS.

Tips for Making Donair Sauce:
1. Chill milk and metal bowl beforehand.
2. Don't use a metal bowl! It will react with the vinegar!
3. Always use a metal bowl.
4. Drizzle vinegar, as you slowly stir.
5. No! Make a whirlpool and add the vinegar all at once!
6. But don't touch it!
7. Ahhh! You broke the sauce! Whisk it vigorously! Panic!
8. Let it sit for a bit. Maybe it will change its mind.
9. Put it into a power mixer, cross yourself, and click your heels three times.
10. Add a little condensed milk, corn starch, mayonnaise, or egg white to thicken it. No one will notice…. Right?

She's a Brick... Sauce

I once heard someone characterize "East Coast donair sauce" as being so thick a spoon will stand up in it, as if you could flip it over like a Dairy Queen blizzard! I found this puzzling, as donair sauce is typically squirted out of a squeeze bottle, which would require it to be a thinner consistency.

I find that donair sauce can range from being a cream of sugar soup, to custard, to something more suited to a mile-high pie. The thickness of donair sauce is fetishized, though, and everyone has their own special technique. Some say a cold metal bowl will produce a thicker sauce. Some say to whisk, while others gasp in horror if you stir more than thrice.

Left: evaporated milk-based donair sauce. Right: sweetened condensed milk-based donair sauce.

Many disgruntled practitioners have turned to using condensed milk as a "cheat". It is foolproof. Your dog could make it. As you stir in the vinegar, you can hear the condensed milk whisper: "You will be assimilated."

While some say this is merely a caricature of true donair sauce, it does have a following. Josh Robinson, from Blowers & Grafton, is a disciple of the condensed scripture. "When I started testing out donair sauces, I tested every different way. I found that I prefer condensed milk. It gives me much more premium flavour." It has a premium price tag too, and, he claims, a certain flavour synergy with the spicy sweat of the meat.

Super Thick (Cheat) Version

1 can (300 ml) sweetened condensed milk
1/3 cup vinegar
1 tsp garlic powder
Just mix it. No skill required.

To Garlic, or Not to Garlic?

Leo Gamoulakos keeps the original recipe, hand-written by his father, folded up in his wallet. He once flashed it before my eyes, but not long enough that I could read it. There were only two things I needed to know, and he was able to confirm them for me: the original recipe was based on evaporated milk (not condensed), and it did contain garlic powder.

The question of the garlic powder had eluded me, as I once worked in a Lunenburg, N.S. pizza shop (ruining many batches of sauce, I will confess) where the sauce was not seasoned in any way. It was simply evaporated milk, sugar, and vinegar. But both garlic and parsley were components of the original sauce, presumably because Peter Gamoulakos fancied it a sweeter, milder version of tzatziki sauce.

The parsley was always fresh parsley, and it was sprinkled on top of the donair rather than being blended into the sauce. The reason for this was that some people didn't like "the green shit" (as I've heard Newfoundlanders refer to it).

Curiously, the garlic used was not fresh, but powdered. Peter McClusky writes in his book, *Ontario Garlic: The Story from Farm to Festival*, that Canadians did not appreciate garlic until immigration laws changed in the '70s.

"Up until then we were a mostly Anglo population with an Anglo appreciation of garlic that was not only very conservative but actually quite negative."

There was a certain stigmatization of garlic. In some areas, children could be sent home from school if they smelled of it! (59)

I have a theory that you are more likely to find sauce sans garlic in rural areas. Jaco Khoury, for example, started omitting the garlic during his stint at Shubie Pizza.

"I'm not a chef," he says. "Whatever recipe they give me, I use. But one time I ran out of garlic and I said, 'Hmm. I'll make it without the garlic.' And I said, 'It's sweet, I kind of like it better.'"

It turned out that his Mi'kmaq customers were also partial to his new recipe, so he's kept it that way ever since.

Types of 'Donair Sauce' across Canada

Sweet Sauce
Simply called "donair sauce" in Atlantic Canada, this is the classic combination of canned milk, sugar, vinegar and garlic. The original recipe calls for evaporated milk, but some restaurants use condensed milk or a mix of the two. In Western Canada, it is sometimes spiked with mayonnaise.

Vegan Donair Sauce
A lot of the vegan restaurants in Halifax substitute the evaporated milk with sweetened condensed coconut milk and cream of coconut.

Keto Donair Sauce
Heavy cream and artificial sweeteners are used.

Garlic Sauce

"Garlic sauce or sweet sauce?" is the question you will be asked at most donair shops outside the Maritimes. But what is garlic sauce, exactly? In Alberta, "garlic sauce" usually refers to a mayonnaise-based sauce with garlic and seasonings.

Tahini Sauce

This sesame paste sauce is flavoured with lemon, garlic and salt. It is the sauce generally used for beef shawarma, so it is only natural that shawarma shops would think to put it on beef donairs.

Sour Cream

Sour cream flavoured with chives and other seasonings is common in northern Alberta. It seems to be a Canadianized version of tzatziki.

Tzatziki

The cucumber yogurt sauce suited to gyros. Some donair shops have a version called "dill sauce", and it is a mix of yogurt, sour cream, dill and other seasonings.

Ranch Dressing

Ranch dressing is a popular dipping sauce in Alberta, and it occasionally finds its way onto donairs.

Hot Sauce

It is common practice in the rest of Canada to put hot chilli sauce on donairs, which is more aligned with how most of the rest of the world eats doner kebab.

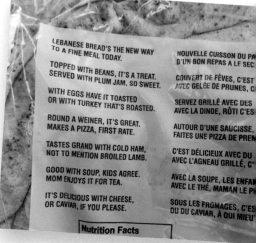

The poem on every bag of Fancy Lebanese Bakery pita bread

The Pita

There is a poem written on every bag of pita bread from the Fancy Lebanese Bakery. Owner Halim Laba once noticed a man out begging in front of the bakery, and commissioned him to write a poem. It's been on the packaging ever since.

Halim opened the bakery in 1962, originally as the Fancy Pastry Shop, specializing in cakes and pastries. As the Lebanese community grew in Halifax, there arose a demand for pita bread, so Halim started baking pita bread at night to have fresh for morning pickup.

Halim died in 1996, and his wife Mary became president.

Mary Laba told *The Coast*, in a special feature, that she would finish the night shift around 4 to 5 a.m., sleep in the office armchair until 9 a.m., and then start the morning shift.

At first, the bakery produced just a couple hundred bags of pita for local families, but nowadays they make a couple hundred thousand, in order to supply all of the grocery stores and restaurants. (60) There is no doubt that the popularity of the donair had something to do with the increased demand.

Flatbreads have been eaten for thousands of years, and are a staple food of Middle Eastern, Balkan and Mediterranean cultures. For millions of people, pita bread is so

The Fancy Lebanese Bakery on Agricola Street.

much more than a novelty bread or donair wrapping paper. It is a staple food, and a symbol of culture and community.

In 2016, Moncton's Fancy Pokket Bakery supplied 900 Syrian refugees with two months of free pita bread, to help with their settlement and orientation.

Owner Mike Timani personally visited families and assisted in whatever ways he could.

"We lived it in Lebanon and we know how difficult that is, you know, the bombing and not knowing who's going to be killed next and where the bomb is going to be thrown," he told CBC Radio Canada. "They felt comfortable, you know. Finally! We've got pita bread." (61)

Timani was born in Venezuela, but his parents moved back to Lebanon when he was five years old. It was his Venezuelan passport that allowed him passage to Canada, when he fled the Lebanese Civil War in 1976. In 1988, he decided to open a restaurant and bakery in Moncton, (61) and now his Fancy Pokket Bakery is the single largest pita producer in Canada. (62)

As for Edmonton, the pita bread of choice comes from the Sunbake Pita Bakery, which also sells a range of Mediterranean pastries and manakeesh.

Breaking Bread

Peter Gamoulakos ran into a bit of a problem when he started making gyros at his restaurant in Bedford. The only pita bakery in town was the Fancy Lebanese Bakery, and they made Arabic-style pita bread. Before he ever thought to change the meat or the sauce, it was the lack of Greek pita bread in Halifax that necessitated the first step of the transformative process leading to the donair.

If Greek pitas had been available in the early '70s, he would have used them, and the donair would be quite different than the one we know today.

Peter would grill the pitas on the flattop in the reddish donair grease from the spit, which imparted flavour and moisture, and made the pita more pliable. This is why the pita seems thicker and chewier than regular warmed pita bread.

As Greek pita bread doesn't have a pocket, Peter Gamoulakos treated the Arabic pitas the same way, placing the toppings on the surface and wrapping with a fold at the bottom. The donair, therefore, is not a stuffed pita, and should not be prepared in that manner.

Extra Sauce

Abe Salloum (of Tony's Donair) worked with Halim, who was his brother-in-law, at the Fancy Lebanese Bakery. Abe would eventually open another Lebanese bakery in 2007: The Golden Bakery on the Bedford Highway. The Golden Bakery (which changed hands in 2018) sells Lebanese pastries and manouche in addition to pita bread.

The process has changed slightly over the years. In previous decades, the meat would be shaved and put onto the grilled pita. Today, the meat must be twice-cooked, so the pita is usually spritzed with a bit of oil and water, and steamed on top of the meat as it grills on the flattop.

Meanwhile in Edmonton, I noticed the pitas being retrieved from steamer drawers. This is a cleaner steam, and the resulting donair is less greasy (for better, or for worse). Grilling the pitas in some sort of fat seems to be a practice that was lost in relocation, oft neglected in any discussion of the "Halifax-style" that fetishizes the sauce at the expense of all the other procedures that originally made the donair uniquely what it is.

Regardless of your area code, there is one solemn, universal rule: Don't ever use a cold pita!

Types of Pita

Turkish Pita
In Turkey, "pide" can refer to pita, "Turkish Pizza" or Ramadan pide (which is traditionally available during Ramadan in Turkey, but is the choice bread for döner kebab in Germany year-round). (63)

Greek Pita
Thick, soft and fluffy with no pocket. This is the type of pita used for gyros and souvlaki.

'Ramadan pide' by pocketcultures is licensed under CC BY 2.0

Arabic Pita
Thin pita with a pocket; the pocket is made when moisture from the dough creates an air bubble as it cooks. This is the type of pita used for shawarma and donair.

Cypriot Pita
An oval-shaped pita with a pocket. It is traditionally cut in half and stuffed with meat. (64)

Lavash
A soft, thin unleavened flatbread, lavash is not, properly speaking, a pita. Lavash is associated with Armenian cuisine, and surrounding areas, and is commonly used for döner kebab in Europe (including Turkey). Some restaurants in Vancouver wrap their donairs in tortilla, as a substitute. (65)

Greek Pita ('Pita' by Nikchick. Licensed under CC BY-SA 2.0).

The toppings bar at PrimeTime Donair in Edmonton.

The Toppings

According to the Halifax purity laws, the only acceptable toppings on a donair are tomatoes and onions. This is the one thing that wasn't altered when the donair underwent its transformation from gyro to donair, when it burst out of its cocoon, into a gooey and misshapen butterfly.

Edmonton has the same standard toppings as Halifax, except for one notorious and controversial addition: lettuce.

I don't think lettuce would survive a voyage on the SS Halifax, with its waterfalls of sticky sauce and greasy tinfoil sauna. There is too much weight, steam, grease, sauce and sweat in the tin zeppelin. The lettuce would die.

But the Edmonton donair carries itself with a little more dignity, at least pretending to be healthy, with its crunchy lettuce and slim fitting pita. It's not scandalous at all to add banana peppers and pickles to your salad. Your sandwich artist will kindly oblige.

The easiest way to understand all of this is to think of the Edmonton donair as a Lebanese hamburger, and to think of the Halifax donair as a Canadian gyro that evolved in pizza shops, and has therefore found its way onto pizza dough and sub buns.

If you leave the Halifax city limits, you'll soon find "super donairs", topped with pepperoni and mozzarella cheese from the pizza bar. You might find these things in Edmonton, too. But the majority of donair shops in Edmonton serve donairs and burgers in combos with fries and pop. Donairs are routinely served with lettuce, tomato, onions and cheese (pickles optional) – you know, stuff you'd find on a hamburger.

It is also fairly common to find donairs served in the fashion of a Philly cheesesteak with sautéed peppers & onions and melted cheese.

Customization is integral to both the hamburger and donair experience in Edmonton, in which simple templates of meat and bread act as creative canvases, and restaurants hold nothing back. If you can put blue cheese on a burger, you can put blue cheese on a donair, and they do just that at High Voltage. At Prime Time Donair, the available toppings include jalapenos, olives and sautéed mushrooms. Customers can also have their meat cooked on the flattop with honey garlic sauce or pineapple curry.

Here are a few crazy signature donairs you'll find in Edmonton:

Eddie's Donair
Philly Melt Cheese Donair: combination of beef donair, cheese, turkey bacon, green peppers, mushrooms, onions, barbecue sauce, mustard, mayo.

Big Bite Pizza & Donair
Fuhgeddaboudit Donair: donair meat, spicy Italian sausage, pepperoni, mozza and pizza sauce.

Glenora Pizza
Butter Chicken Donair: chicken, lettuce, tomatoes, onions, cheese and butter chicken donair sauce.

Vegas Donair & Poutine
BLVD Donair: beef, lettuce, pickles, cheese and Treasure Island Sauce.

King of Donair
Hot Blonde: pineapple, hot peppers, cheese and Dave's hot sauce. Wait – what?! It would seem that since opening in Edmonton, King of Donair has caught the creative bug and brought it back to Halifax!

Travel Blogger Cailin O'Neil tries out the hand-held method (From: Travel Yourself).

How to Eat It

When Peter Gamoulakos served his first donairs, people weren't sure how to eat them. "Peel back the foil and eat like an ice cream cone," he told them.

This may seem obvious to an Edmontonian, but it is a difficult task to eat a Halifax donair in this fashion. The Halifax donair, with its tremendous amount of meat and sauce, and absurdly small pita, defies the very act of being eaten.

Donair Eating Methods
Hand-held (Version 1): The original way a donair was intended to be eaten. Peel off the wrapper, and eat it like a burrito. Make sure to lean forward.

Hand-held (Version 2): If the donair is too big and clumsy to "eat like an ice cream cone," you can pick out pieces of meat with your hands, and continue eating this way until the donair deflates. Once the pita fits around the meat, revert to Version 1.

Hand-held (Version 3): Sauce on the side. This allows you to control the sauce factor, and makes the donair much easier to pick up and eat. You can just drizzle a bit of sauce before taking each bite. There are many advocates of this technique, while others criticize it for detracting from the "authentic donair experience".

Open-faced (Version 1): If your donair comes served on a plate (or you've transported it to a plate), and cutlery is available, you can make a civilized attempt to fork 'n knife it. Keep in mind, however, that cutlery is strictly forbidden by donair purists.

From North City Donair's video tutorial: "How to Eat a Donair"

Open-faced (Version 2): If your donair is wrapped in foil, open it up to expose the beauty within. It is perfectly acceptable to eat with your hands. Start by picking strips of meat off the top, and once you can see the pita, tear pieces off to eat with the meat.

Family Style: Order a side of grilled pitas and use them to eat an open-faced donair, as you would injera or naan bread. (Travel blogger Cailin O'Neil came up with this when we were confronted with a particularly large "research donair" at Robert's Pizza).

The best way to enjoy a donair is right in the pizza shop, where everything is fresh, and you can notice little touches like a slight crisp to the pita, the consistency of the sauce or the plating.

Whether you are enjoying an Edmonton donair or a Halifax donair, you are enjoying a uniquely Canadian food. We should overcome our interprovincial bickering and be proud of the donair in all its shapes and forms. On the other hand, why should Haligonians allow outsiders to pervert their local delicacy? Should they not rage into the night, like the Quebecois, who clutch their curds every time an Anglo province commits some travesty against their proud poutines?

Is there not a case for the truly authentic donair?

6

The Authentic Donair

"My first exposure to a donair was in 1977 when, as a student in broadcasting school, the donair was my primary source of sustenance for well over eight months. Every day before heading off to learn my trade, I would stop in at King of Donair on Quinpool Road and spend, as I recall, under $3 for a single donair with hot peppers, parsley and a squeeze of lemon washed down by an ice-cold Brio Chinotto. (Totally old school)." – Jordi Morgan, in "An Open Letter to Mayor and Council on the Donair Debate." (66)

While the rest of Canada runs wild and free with a loose definition of donair, Halifax is a gated community by comparison.

Earlier this year, someone with the online alias RangerNS put forth a proposal to the Halifax subreddit (i.e. the Halifax forum within the social sharing website, Reddit) that would forbid the misrepresentation of donairs on the online forum. Penalties would range from gentle shaming to lifetime bans from the community.

Rule VI Donairs are Donairs. Mis-Identification is forbidden.

Describing non-donairs as donairs is incorrect and dishonourable to this great culinary development, and to the culture and people of Halifax. As such, it is forbidden in r/Halifax

Donair consists of: Pita bread steamed and fried before preparing; wrapping strips of: donair meat, a highly spiced meat loaf, mostly of ground beef, lamb and pork, formed on a spit, baked, heated and fried before serving; donair sauce: evaporated milk, sugar, vinegar and garlic powder; and, optionally: chopped onions and chopped tomato. Any other topping excludes it from being called a donair.

In the comments, people made cases for cheese, French fries, banana peppers and even lettuce.

"I've had cheese on donairs for 30 years. If it's on the menu everywhere under toppings = acceptable. Not taking tips from someone who thinks pork belongs in donair meat," snarked user SolonGoose.

A regular donair at King of Donair. (Photo: Cailin O'Neil)

There was a call-to-action from Fatboyhfx:

"Free yourselves from the shackles of the donair puritans."

The underground resistance, veiled in the safety of anonymity, emerged in this discussion forum, proving that not everyone in Halifax adheres to, or even cares about, the so-called purity laws. But there has been a long-established tradition of Nova Scotians barking at their fellow Canadians about the mishandling of their precious donair. Inevitably, that troublesome word is uttered.

"That's not an *authentic* donair."

This is confusing to people in the western provinces because, as far as they are concerned, an "authentic donair" would be what you are served in Turkey.

But to a Nova Scotian, the donair is not a synonym for "doner". It is an expression of the doner kebab that came into existence within a specific time, place and cultural context. It is uniquely ours, just as Philadelphia has the cheese steak and Washington has the half smoke. Some say the Halifax donair should have protected status, like how the Associazione Verace Pizza Napoletana protects Naples-style pizza.

Then again, such adherence to the purity laws could cause stagnation and cease innovation, thereby denying the world unforeseen deliciousness. There needs to be compromise. Besides, the donair *has* been changing, right before our eyes.

The Evolution

The first problem with "authenticity" is that the donair has evolved over time, and what we consider "authentic" now may not align with the original intention.

Take the example of the clubhouse sandwich: most people assume that the defining characteristic of the clubhouse is the double-decker construction, when, in fact, the original clubhouse sandwiches were not double decker.

One of the earliest recipes is from The Union Club in New York in 1889: "Two toasted slices of Graham bread, with a layer of turkey or chicken and ham between them, served warm."

There are some purists who condemn the double-decker version. Among them, the great James Beard, who referred to them as a "three-decker" and wrote in his ground-breaking *James Beard's American Cookery*: "Nowadays the sandwich is bastardized because it is usually made as a three-decker, which is not authentic (whoever started that horror should be forced to eat three-deckers three times a day the rest of his life)."

Plated donair at Panada Pizza (Halifax): the parsley garnish pays tribute to the original recipe.

When Peter Gamoulakos started serving donairs at Velos Souvlakia, he intended for them to resemble Greek gyros as much as Canadianly possible, using ground lamb and tzatziki sauce. The only thing he didn't have was Greek pita bread.

The invention story condenses years of evolution into a quick soundbite, as if the whole recipe came to Peter all at once, and yogurt was banned by an ordinance from city government.

The truth is that Peter Gamoulakos was selling donairs, with varying ratios of lamb to beef, for many months before he sweetened the deal. The truth is that tzatziki sauce would continue to be popular, long after Peter developed donair sauce, especially among his Greek customers. So, if we're talking authenticity, well, you can't get more authentic than that!

The donair has evolved over time to become what it is today, and it's still evolving. Is there a time in history when the donair was most authentic? Was it 1974, 1987 or 2005?

Did the donair blossom into a fully developed thing with Peter Gamoulakos, or has it been altered by every hand that touched it? Is authenticity tied to a specific place, a time of day, or, for that matter, a state of consciousness?

Is the donair you ate at Pizza Corner in 1992 the same as the donair you vaguely remember from last night? The more we try to define the donair, or limit it, the more it oozes around the edges, dripping through our fingers.

Trying to capture authenticity is like trying to go home. Remember the first time you came home to visit after university (or the oil patch, or "finding yourself" overseas) and everything was different? You drive the same loops, and sit on the same rocks, but it's not the same. Had you never left, you probably wouldn't have experienced this disruption. It's always been like this. Nothing has changed. The petals fall to the soil, but you don't recall there ever being a flower there.

Here is a list of supposed changes to the Halifax donair since 1974:

Tzatziki was originally a perfectly acceptable, even more authentic, sauce for the donair.

"*We* didn't eat the sweet sauce, we used tzatziki. But people would order a donair with a cup of that sauce on the side and it would be running down their elbows, and we were like, I can't believe they're eating that stuff!" – Mike Nicoletopoulos, on growing up in a Greek family with a donair shop (Island Greek, in Sydney).

(Opposite) Owner Justin Ayre of Alexandra's Pizza (Sydney) holding a 12-pound donair. A cash prize was promised to anyone who could consume the colossal donair in 90 minutes. - Photo by Chris Connors/THE CAPE BRETON POST

A donair with parsley from Mezza. This is one of the few donair shops in Halifax to offer parsley as a topping.

"The public liked the sweet sauce more on the donair, but the Greek people in Halifax used to order tzatziki. Some people requested tahini. But in Canada now, the most popular is the sweet sauce. I used to sell cups of that sauce, like a 16-ounce cup for Coke." – Charles Smart

Donairs used to be smaller.
It should probably be no surprise that portion sizes have been steadily increasing over the years. We live in a supersized world of Big Gulps and "belly busters", but everything was generally smaller back in the day. Even a small donair today is quite the feast, and the biggest dump truck of a donair can easily exceed two pounds.

"I remember the idea of a small donair was legitimately a small donair. It was very small, like a couple bites. Some places used to do like 10 small donairs for 15 bucks and we'd eat five or six or seven. … Belly busters came out of nowhere. All of a sudden donairs increased in popularity and people wanted the craziest donairs they could get." - Neil MacFarlane (donair enthusiast)

"If I make a donair for somebody in my house it'll taste different than what people expect nowadays, and not because I'm some sort of culinary genius, but because I don't overload it. It's not supposed to have six pounds of meat and 16 pounds of sauce. It's supposed to have a little bit of everything so you get a taste of everything." – Mike Nicoletopoulos (Greek Fest/Pizza Corner veteran)

There was parsley.
Fresh parsley was an original ingredient but it is now extremely rare to find a donair shop that still sprinkles parsley on after the sauce.

The meat was house-made.
Before the mid-'90s, most shops made their own donair meat, and reputations would ride on the quality and flavour of the meat. Today, the majority of donair shops get their meat from the same handful of wholesalers.

It wasn't as spicy.
I am told that the original spice blend was closer in nature to gyro spices, which are milder than some of the spice bombs around Halifax. King of Donair and Mr. Donair are more "authentic" in this sense, while pretty much every Lebanese restaurateur I've spoken to has said, "When I took over, I added more flavour." Some shops have spicier donair meat than others, which is really a matter of personal taste.

The meat was not twice-cooked.
The original method of making donairs was to shave the meat off the spit and place it directly on the pita. But after the health scares of 2004 and 2006, the Canadian government mandated that donair and shawarma shops twice-cook their meat. Donair meat is shaved off the spit and grilled on the flattop, which has the effect of making it crispier (which many people enjoy). In fact, before the Donair Working Group's recommendations, there were already pizza shops following the practice, and customers who would request their meat "extra crispy". Donair purists, however, insist that the meat should never go on the grill.

"I love the burnt edges, like brisket burnt ends at a BBQ restaurant – that's what grilled donair meat reminds me of." – Omar Mouallem

The meat was certainly not pre-sliced or sliced and frozen.
An unfortunate trend of the last decade has been to pre-slice the meat and store it in a steam table pan or warmer drawer until the dinner rush.

The Canadian government also has precise recommendations on how to freeze leftover donair meat, which sometimes requires slicing and freezing the meat. (49)

"Once the meat is on the machine, you must sell it that same day. Otherwise, throw it out – it's good for nothing else." – Peter Gamoulakos in 1978 (28)

Electronic donair slicer at North City Donair in Prince George, BC. From North City Donair (Facebook)

King Of Donair @KingOfDonair · May 31, 2017
Pineapple 🍍 FTW!
#novascotia #donairs #halifax #donair #instafood #nomnomnom
#edmonton #calgary #foodporn #foodnetwork #foodbeast #foodies

💬 1   ⟲ 2   ♡ 18   ⬆️

King of Donair promoting pineapple as a donair topping on their Twitter feed.

There is a difference, of course, between adding a topping versus changing everything that makes a donair a donair. Here is a riddle: What is the unifying concept of every donair, the one thing that all donairs have, and that you can't add or subtract without losing the donair? Let's face it: Using the word "donair" as an umbrella term for any pita-wrapped kebab has become ingrained in Canadian tradition. The language police are over at the Burger Baron, eating cheesy chicken donairs and there's nothing you can do about it.

This Canadian donair discrepancy, between the East and West, reminds me of how souvlaki, in Athens, has come to mean any kind of pita sandwich, whereas in northern Greece, it specifically means grilled meat on a skewer.

Or, how döner kebab is the name for the meat in Turkey, but has been co-opted to mean a sandwich in Germany.

Since Canada seems to have adopted the word "donair" to refer to a range of pita-wrapped kebabs, perhaps instead of gatekeeping what is and isn't a donair, we should instead acknowledge regional variations and styles across Canada.

After all, if you've been following along, you may have realized by now that the Edmonton donair is, in some ways, closer to Peter Gamoulakos's original intention than the sloppy sweet donairs ruling present-day Halifax.
Have we come full circle?

Types of Donair

The Halifax Donair

In Halifax, the word "donair" means one thing: spicy minced beef loaf shaved off a vertical spit and served in a grilled pita with onions, tomato and donair sauce (canned milk, sugar, vinegar). Halifax donairs are VERY meat-heavy, and the vegetables are merely garnish. Visitors from other provinces are sometimes shocked when they order a large donair, thinking that it will be a reasonable size, but instead are presented with an absurdly heavy package.

While the sweet sauce and spicy beef most typify the Halifax donair, you can't just put donair sauce on a gyro and call it "donair". There is a dedicated process from start to finish that creates something much more than the sum of its parts.

In an old Chow Hound post, a disgruntled Haligonian (wise to the ways of donair) detailed the struggle of ordering a "Halifax-style" donair from a shop in Vancouver:
> *This is what happened:*
> *- I order.*
> *- He gets out a full dry pita and opens it up to make a pouch. WRONG*
> *- He puts in large wedges of tomatoes. WRONG*
> *- He puts in diced onions. RIGHT*
> *- He then turns around and shovels out of a hot bowl the sliced anemic beef and stuffs it into the pocket of the pita. WRONG*
> *- Pulls out a white squeeze bottle and squeezed something into the pocket. WRONG*

A large donair from Randy's Pizza, without sauce. If you look carefully, you can see the pita bread.

- Then he folds it all up into a tightly packed ball and hands it to me. WRONG
- All of this took about 25 seconds.
I left cringing.
Then our anonymous internet expert goes on to explain in perfect detail how to make a proper Halifax donair:
- Slice the properly flavourful and spiced pressed beef from the spit.
- Place the pile of sliced meat on the hot flat oven plate.
- Spray the meat with water and/or oil.
- Mix the meat. This will cook the meat further and provide the golden brown colour of the meat and seal in the flavours.
- Place a pita that is sized to the order (small, medium, large), whole, on top of the meat on the grill.
- Spray the pita and meat again with water/oil. Not too much.
- Place a flat tray, or pan, over the meat and the pita to trap the juices and flavour.
- Remove the pita and mix up the meat. The pita should be warm and slightly moist.
- Move to another station and lay the pita down and place the meat on it, then layer the diced onions and diced tomatoes on it.
- Ask the client how much sauce they want.
- Ladle the appropriate amount of the signature Halifax donair sauce over the meat and vegetables.
- Wrap up the pita with a fold at the bottom and then in a round so that the top is open.
- Wrap the whole thing tightly in tinfoil.
- Give to customer

It should take about three or four minutes.
If you don't do these steps above, don't ever call it a Halifax Donair.

If you've ever wondered which wines pair best with a donair, here are some recommendations from sommelier James Gallant:

"For a white wine I would definitely look to something with a bit of sweetness so I would look to something like a Riesling. Something with a bit of residual sugar that cuts through the donair sauce, which is a curve ball in this pairing. On the red side I would probably go for a California red. I would be looking for a Merlot or maybe a Zinfandel, something that's going to have a little bit of sweetness but that's still going to cut through the donair sauce while playing well with the spices from the donair meat."

Vegan Donair from Real Fake Meats in Halifax.

Edmonton-style donair from 'Simon King' in Edmonton.

The Super Donair
A donair with pepperoni and mozzarella cheese, which is especially popular in Pictou County.

The Vegan Donair
There are at least five restaurants in Halifax with vegan donairs, as I write this, but I would guess that many more are on the way as plant-based options are becoming increasingly popular. Seitan is spiced like donair meat, and the sauce is typically made of condensed coconut milk.

The Edmonton Donair
This donair is made from the same spit-shaved meat, and the same sweet sauce as its Halifax counterpart. Some reports say that the beef is less spicy, or that the sauce is less sweet, but this varies from shop to shop in each city.

The Edmonton donair embodies the Albertan spirit of individual freedom. Edmontonians don't like anyone telling them how to eat their donairs; they have no use for laws or regulations, and will challenge tradition.

When you order a donair in Edmonton you will be asked: "lettuce, tomato, onion, sweet sauce, cheese?" But ordering takes on a Subway-esque approach, in which the donair is customized to personal taste. It is entirely acceptable to add pickles, sautéed peppers and alternative sauces (you might be asked, "sweet or garlic?").

Chicken donair from Donair Dude in Vancouver. This is something you won't see in Halifax, unless, of course, it's shawarma.

Donairs on the grill at Vancouver's Donair Dude. (From Facebook).

The pita is steamed, not grilled in grease, and is tightly wrapped. A durable tinfoil with a paper lining is used, often in combination with a plastic bag. While a Halifax donair generally has excess meat hanging out the end, the Edmonton donair is more prone to excess pita bread. The goal, though, is to have a balance of ingredients in every bite.

The Chicken Donair

Every donair shop in Edmonton has a chicken donair on the menu, but unlike "beef donairs" the poultry version resembles a spit of shawarma. Chicken donairs are quite rare in Halifax, usually sold by restaurants that already offer shawarma, and may or may not be called donair or even listed on the menu. Uncle Buck's calls theirs a "Zesty Chicken Pita", for example. Greco and Johnny K's both serve chicken donairs made from ground chicken, rather than a shawarma-style stack. In 2020 King of Donair announced that they are adding chicken mince donairs to their repertoire as well.

The Mix Donair

A mix of chicken and beef donair in the same pita – this is popular in Edmonton.

The Grilled Donair

There is a vague style of donair common to Calgary and Vancouver, which I like to call the "shawarma donair" or the "burrito donair". In some locales, the word donair indicates the type of meat used, while in others it refers to any type of filling (including falafel) wrapped in a pita. It is sometimes made in the fashion of a stuffed pita, or rolled up in a tortilla. There is an even ratio of pickles/salad to meat. The wrap is grilled on a panini press and wrapped in paper. There will sometimes be a "Halifax option", which refers to the sauce rather than the style.

Donair Spin-offs

Classic Scotian Pizza Shop Fare

It is common for Halifax pizza shops to have extensive menus, and in addition to pizza and donairs, you can expect to see: subs, poutine, garlic fingers, nachos, fried seafood, fried chicken, burgers, pita wraps, wings, salad, pasta, fried pepperoni and other apps, and typically a clubhouse sandwich.

It is not that common to see souvlaki or shawarma served alongside donairs, which aren't associated with kebab shops like in most other locales.

While there are some shops that have a Mediterranean flair, others specialize in slice slingin', extreme pizza concepts or family-style fish 'n chips. Some pizza shops just seem to specialize in non-specialization! Due to this culture of variety, the donair has found its way into many other dishes at your one-stop local pizza shop. Here are a few mainstays:

Garlic Fingers: A pizza dough base is slathered with garlic butter and loaded with mozzarella. After baking, it is cut into "fingers". Similar dishes are found in other regions (Wisconsin, for example, calls them "cheese fries" or "pizza fries") but what makes this dish truly Nova Scotian is the default donair dipping sauce.

Garlic fingers from Kit Kat Pizza with lots of donair dipping sauce.

A bubba sub from A-1 Pizza in Liverpool, N.S. (Photo: Vernon Oickle)

Donair Pizza: Since virtually every pizza shop serves donair, it only makes sense that donair pizza is a thing. It contains donair meat, mozzarella, onion and tomatoes. Donair sauce is usually ladled on top after baking.

Donair Panzerotti (or Calzone): The next logical step is to make folded pizzas with donair ingredients, what is sometimes called "Donairzerotti". In Cape Breton they have similar dishes called "pizza flips" (or donair flips) and "ponzos".

Donair Sub: Oven-baked subs are served at most Maritime pizza shops, and the donair sub is popular partly because it is easier to eat than a donair. It is also characterized by being baked in the oven with mozzarella cheese.

Bubba Sub: This is a variation of the donair sub that is said to have been started in Yarmouth, Nova Scotia. There was a guy named "Bubba" (a regional nickname for "buddy") who requested a donair sub without vegetables. He asked the pizza shop to spread both sides of the bun with garlic butter, and bake it with donair meat and cheese. There's a spattering of pizza shops that also serve Bubba pizzas.

Hero Sub: A toasted sub with pepperoni, ham, salami, donair meat, lettuce, tomatoes and mozzarella. This is a specialty of Cape Breton.

Donair Plate: French fries are topped with donair meat and baked in a tinfoil plate with cheese. Tomatoes, onions and sauce are then added.

Donair Poutine from Cheese Curds (Photo: Amy Langdon)

Donair Pogo: Yes, it is a corn dog with a tube of donair meat inside.

Donair Poutine: The classic pizza shop version is a travesty of frozen fries, shredded mozza and donair meat drenched in gravy. Nowadays there are plenty of places offering proper poutine with hand-cut fries and cheese curds. Depending on the restaurant, donair sauce, tomatoes and onions may or may not feature in the donair poutine.

Donair Nachos: Many pizza shops in Halifax have nachos on the menu, and since it's Halifax, of course we put donair meat on our nachos.

Donair Burger: In Nova Scotia, a donair burger RARELY ever means a hamburger topped with donair meat. Instead, it is donair meat, sauce and veggies in a hamburger bun. It was likely introduced in Cape Breton, where the "pizza burger" was already popular. (A Cape Breton pizza burger is a hamburger bun filled with pepperoni, cheese and pizza sauce).

Donair egg rolls from Dino's Pizza (web site), Summerside, P.E.I.

Donair Egg Rolls: This is a more recent phenomenon. I first noticed these around 2009, but I'm actually not sure when or where they originated. Nowadays it seems as though everyone is serving them.

At the grocery store: The **Donair Kit** is found in grocery stores across the country, and has been a staple in Atlantic Canada for years. Vacuum-sealed slices of donair meat are sold with pita bread and a packet of donair sauce. They are primarily sold by Bonté Foods and Mr. Donair (and their associated brands). Donair sauce is also sold in squeeze bottles. Another item you might find in the grocery aisle is the **donair sausage**. Mr. Donair is the largest producer, but various local butcher shops also make encased meats with donair spices.

The Halifax donair obsession is not limited to pizza shops, and you will find donair-inspired dishes all over the city. Whereas in Edmonton, the donair is treated more like a hamburger, with different toppings and combinations creatively applied to the donair template, Haligonians are staunchly opposed to meddling with the "authentic" recipe.

Halifax, however, has no problem incorporating the donair into other foods, and there is no limit to the absurdity that would likely raise an Edmonton eyebrow. Here are all of the donair spin-offs (to my knowledge) that have graced the city of Halifax:

Donair Doughnut
Robie Street Station & Tony's Donair (Donair Crawl 2015)
The donair doughnut (a.k.a. the doughnairnut) was famously served during the inaugural donair crawl of 2015. Robie Street Station is a brunch specialty restaurant next to Tony's Donair, so the two restaurants combined forces to make the doughnairnut

Donair Cheesecake (Credit: Dagley Media).

a reality. A yeast doughnut was topped with a glaze made from Tony's donair sauce, and the doughnut was topped with Tony's donair meat, and diced tomatoes and green onions.

Donair Cheesecake
Sweet Hereafter (Donair Crawl 2016)
The Sweet Hereafter is a cheesecake specialty shop on Quinpool Road, and they participated in the Second Donair Crawl (2016) with their donair cheesecake.

A shortbread crust supported donair sauce-infused cream cheese filling and morsels of donair meat. It was topped with onions and tomatoes and drizzled with donair sauce.

Donair Cupcake (National Donair Day 2018)
Susie's Shortbreads
This cupcake specialty bakery made a special batch of donair cupcakes, in collaboration with King of Donair, for National Donair Day (December 8). Vanilla cake was baked with donair meat in it, and was topped with donair sauce-cream cheese frosting and sundried tomato sprinkles. It was served at the bakery and at King of Donair.

Donair Gelato
Humani-T Café (Natal Day 2011)
Neighbourhood café and gelato slinger, Humani-T made donair gelato just once, as a stunt for Natal Day (a civic holiday celebrating the "birth" of Halifax).

Donair Gnocci at aFrite Restaurant.

Donair Sushi Burrito
Where to find it: Way2Roll
The sushi burrito trend finally caught on in Halifax in 2017 with the opening of Way2Roll. A sushi burrito is essentially a giant sushi roll that is eaten like a burrito, and when in Rome (or Halifax, as the case may be) there's going to be a donair option. Way2Roll moved into sister restaurant, Kyo Kitchen, which serves the Halifax Roll: donair meat, lettuce, tomato, onion, cream cheese and donair sauce wrapped up in rice and nori. There is also a poke bowl option.

Donair Tartare
Where to find it: The Stubborn Goat
The Stubborn Goat has had donair tartare on their menu sporadically over the years. Chopped raw beef and donair spices are drizzled with donair sauce and served with crispy pita and cucumber slices.

Donair New Zealand Pot Pies
Where to find it: Humble Pie Kitchen
Dartmouth's Humble Pie makes delectable New Zealand-style pot pies, which are butter flake pastry hand pies. They make their own donair meat, and fill up their pastry with meat, tomatoes, onion and a garlicky sweet donair sauce.

Donair Hot Dog
Where to find it: Cheese Curds
Cheese Curds is known for its gourmet burgers and poutines, but they have dabbled in the fine art of hot doggery, even rolling out a food truck specializing in hot dogs and poutine. The donair hot dog is, you guessed it, a hot dog with donair meat, sauce and fixins.

Donair Stuffed Pan Rolls
Where to find it: Devine Dishes
Devine Dishes is a catering and gourmet take-away shop located in Dartmouth. Every Friday they make stuffed pan rolls, with donair meat and ooey gooey cheese. Sauce on the side.

Donair Lasagna
Where to find it: Dallas Pizza & Steak House, Sir Donair
Despite all odds, this is actually found at a few places in Edmonton.

Donair Caesar (Drink)
Where to find it: Blowers & Grafton, aFrite Restaurant

Donair tartare at The Roof Top (by the Stubborn Goat).

Recipe: Donair Clubhouse

This is my own recipe that I came up with when I was brainstorming this list. I thought: "I've never heard of anyone doing a donair clubhouse. That's surprising." So I took matters into my own hands. With any clubhouse sandwich, the "recipe" is more about making sure complementary ingredients are paired in the same layers. This sandwich was so delicious, I was asked to make it for dinner the next day. You can use pre-cooked chicken breast, and donair meat from your favourite shop, or you can make all, or some, of it from scratch. Enjoy.

Recipe — DONAIR CLUBHOUSE

Ingredients

3 PIECES OF WHITE BREAD, TOASTED

SLICED DONAIR MEAT

COOKED & SLICED CHICKEN BREAST

(OR TURKEY)

EQUAL PARTS DONAIR SAUCE AND

MAYONNAISE, MIXED

SLICED TOMATO

SLICED ONION

LETTUCE

Directions

START WITH A PIECE OF TOAST, SPREAD WITH THE SAUCE.

FIRST LAYER: ONIONS AND DONAIR MEAT.

TOP WITH A PIECE OF SAUCED TOAST.

NEXT LAYER: SAUCE, CHICKEN, TOMATOES, LETTUCE.

TOP WITH A PIECE OF SAUCED TOAST.

STICK TOOTHPICKS INTO EACH QUADRANT, AND SLICE SANDWICH INTO FOUR.

(Right) The Donair Clubhouse

7

The Great Canadian Donair Trail

Whether you are a donair tourist, a homesick Maritimer, or drunk and hungry in an unfamiliar city, beckoned by that sweet siren song, this list is your donair resource. I have not been to every one of these places, so these are not restaurant reviews or necessarily my top picks. Instead, I have tried to document the story of the donair across Canada and how it has touched lives, how it has become a local fixture, embedded into our foodways at different contextual and cultural cross-points, how it has become a symbolic template for national identity.

(It's actually just a list of donair shops across Canada, guys). Feel free to extrapolate or simply salivate. Just pass the sauce.

Halifax Legends

Halifax is where it all began, and the city is soaking and dripping in both history and deliciousness. Make sure to check out these legendary donair shops.

Randy's Pizza
2380 Agricola St, Halifax and others
Open since 1987, Randy's has legions of fans addicted to its well-endowed, expertly made donairs. In addition to its Agricola St. flagship store, there are locations in downtown Dartmouth and Lower Sackville.

King of Donair
6420 Quinpool Rd., Halifax
King of Donair is the original Halifax donair shop. The Quinpool Road location is the oldest and most iconic of the franchise, which now has five locations in Halifax: Quinpool, Dartmouth, Clayton Park, Sackville and the Scotiabank Centre (so you can enjoy a donair at a Mooseheads game). The walls are covered in photos and articles, so you can soak up the history before you soak up the donair.

Tony's Donair.

King of Donair is known for their marketing antics, from hilarious and controversial advertising stunts, to festive promotions, celebrity sightings and eating challenges.

Tony's Donair
2390 Robie St., Halifax

Tony's Donair is one of the most iconic restaurants in Halifax, with its neon glow beckoning hungry locals from across the Halifax Common. The sign proudly claims, "Since 1976", but less known is that Tony's was originally a Mr. Donair, of the fledgling Gamoulakos chain. The store was renamed when it was acquired by Abe Salloum and Tony Helou. It is widely known as being one of the best donairs in Halifax.

Revana Pizza
29 Portland St., Dartmouth

Revana Pizza was opened in 1977 by Chawki El-Homeira (aka Charles Smart). That's right: the guy who introduced the donair to Edmonton was also the first to introduce the donair to Dartmouth! But Chawki would leave Nova Scotia before the end of the decade, selling Revana to one of his employees, Jack Toulany.

When I chatted with Jack Toulany, he told me that he was only a teenager when he first arrived in Halifax, and his cousin took him for a drive to show him around the city. This is when he was introduced to his first donair at Tony's, where the young Jack would end up getting a job.

"The first week I worked there, we got robbed," Jack says. "Two guys came in with a shotgun and robbed us. They had the shotgun pointed at me first. Buddy wouldn't open the cash so they beat him up with the gun. I ran to the back room to outside, trying to ask for help, but I didn't speak English."

Despite having this traumatic experience, Jack decided to go into business for himself. Tony Helou encouraged Jack to "buy from Chawki," himself a former Tony's employee, who was now looking to sell his Dartmouth shop.

"Everything was good and the bank gave me money," says Jack, "But when the bank saw my ID they said, 'I'm sorry, we don't give money to minors.

You need someone to co-sign for you.'"

He was 17.

Jack's recipe is a highly guarded secret, and he says people have tried to steal it over the years. He even started posting fake recipes on the kitchen bulletin board, to derail would-be recipe thieves. Even relatives have been guilty.

"I once told a relative that I would give him the spices to use, so he brought unopened spices to see how much I took out when making the spices for him."

Revana Pizza is a staple of downtown Dartmouth, and is conjoined to Whiskey's Lounge, where you can enjoy a cold one with your historic meal.

Mezza Lebanese Cuisine (formally Venus Pizza)
1558 Barrington St., Halifax and other locations
A 1974 advertisement in the Yellow Pages for Venus Pizza (2764 Gottingen St.) indicates a specialization in spaghetti, ravioli and lasagna. I'm not sure who originally opened it, but it went through several ownership changes. In the late 1970s, the restaurant

Venus Pizza on Barrington St. before the rebrand.

Extra Sauce ..

was owned by Eva and George Sayde (sister and brother-in-law to Abe Salloum of Tony's Donair). It was then sold to Victor Habib in the early 1990s, whose father-in-law Norman Nahas, opened a second location on Barrington Street, in Halifax's downtown.

A few years later they would sell both locations to Elias Nahas (Norman's brother).

Elias Nahas, as you might remember from chapter 3, bought the Tony's Donair in the Halifax Shopping Centre in 1990. When the 10-year contract was up, Elias aligned the food court stall with his Venus restaurants.

Venus Pizza now had restaurants on Gottingen Street, Barrington Street, and the Halifax Shopping Centre. The focus shifted from pastas and subs toward donairs, shawarma and Lebanese food. It was the first restaurant in Halifax to serve shawarma.

Eventually the Gottingen Street location was sold (it now houses Shadia's Pizza), but the Venus on Barrington Street, which was just a couple of blocks away from Pizza Corner, and open just as late, became iconic. It's where I would go if I wanted my donair served by a singing Lebanese man with a side of stuffed grape leaves.

In 2006, Elias opened Mezza Mediterranean Grill, serving Lebanese food with waiters and ambiance on Quinpool Road, west of the Halifax Common.

The family business now consisted of the Venus flagship store, its food court sister restaurant, and an upscale model. They were all successful, but there wasn't a cohesive brand.

When Elias retired, he handed the reins to his sons, who had grown up washing dishes, prepping and cooking at the family restaurants. When Peter and Tony Nahas took control in 2012 they decided to rebrand as a fast-casual chain: Mezza Lebanese Kitchen. (67)

Mezza Lebanese Kitchen is a spruced-up, streamlined rebrand of Venus that has been wildly successful. The first prototype was opened in Dartmouth's Burnside business park in 2012, and there are now 12 locations in Nova Scotia, including the iconic Barrington Street store.

While I miss the old Venus, (which, in my opinion, had more grit, more character, more soul), Mezza has done a great job marketing itself to a new generation for healthy, fresh and fast meals.

Robert's Famous Pizza & Donairs
364 Windmill Rd., Dartmouth

Robert's first opened "underneath the bridge" in the late '70s or early '80s. It has changed locations a couple of times, but has always been a fixture of north-end Dartmouth, with a cult-like following for its gigantic donairs.

When I asked how many people the Belly Buster would feed, I was told: "Seven … or eight? It depends how hungry you are."

The other thing that stood out to me about Robert's was the bullet holes in the front window. When I inquired, owner Malek Badour, who says he took over the shop in the late '80s, shrugged: "It could happen anywhere."

"Super-size Donair from Robert's Pizza Donairs & Subs.

In the early days, Robert's served all the nearby military housing and was incredibly busy. I am told that on a weekend there would be eight or nine people working the grill, and you could barely get in the door. It was so busy, in fact, that the meat didn't have enough time to cook, so (I am told) they would cut the half-cooked meat off the spit and throw it in a stainless steel pan full of boiling water. The result was not ideal, to say the least, and Robert's still hasn't shaken off the "boiled meat" stigma.

However, a trip to Robert's today is quite different from the crazy '90s. When I visited, in the winter of 2020, the military housing, which had long been a ghost town, was torn down, and there was a single spinning donair cone, glistening with steam and grease. Robert's still does things the old-fashioned way, making the donair meat by hand and slicing it with an old school knife (you can rest assured that there is no boiling step). Malek says he likes to treat his meat like shawarma, slicing it unevenly, so that there are thick, meaty chunks and crispy bits. According to Robert's fans, there is nothing else like it.

Euro Pizza
293 St. Margarets Bay Rd., Halifax

Nick Giannopoulos earned his chops back in the late '80s at PG's, Peter Gamoulakos's post-KOD restaurant in Spryfield. In 1987, he opened European Food Shop, a founding member of Pizza Corner, and the first in Halifax to serve pizza slices. People would line up down the street for slices and it became too crazy. So, Nick sold the shop, did some catering and travelled around Europe for a bit.

Then in 1998, he opened Euro Pizza. He prides himself on his original recipe donair, using Peter Gamoulakos's spices (i.e. Mr. Donair brand meat). He uses olive oil from Greece, makes his own yogurt for his tzatziki sauce, and makes his pita bread from scratch.

Donair from Euro Pizza.

"They used to say, who is that crazy dude selling pizza slices? I was 27. I was a crazy youngster back then, now I'm a crazy man. I'm the crazy old man that does that. I'm just passionate about food, that's all. I've always made pitas in-house. I've made homemade yogurt every morning for the last 22 years."

Pizza Time
731 Pleasant St., Dartmouth
For most of Pizza Time's 35-plus-year history, Camille and Rima Toulany were at the helm, and Pizza Time has become one of the most beloved (and busy) neighbourhood pizza shops in the Halifax region. There is only enough room inside to pick up an order, but you are welcomed, (and possibly offered a treat), while the half dozen staff perform a ballet of organized chaos.

Camille and Rima decided to retire in 2018 when family friend Chris Jebailey showed interest in taking the Eastern Passage gem off their hands. Chris was working as a commercial banker at the time, but had tired of crunching numbers. He says he's too much of an extrovert, and craved a livelihood that involved people, food, community and hands-on work. After the Toulanys returned from a vacation to Lebanon, they told Chris, who had been caring for the shop in their absence, "How about now?"
For Chris, it was Pizza Time!

Over the next two weeks, Chris quit his job and learned everything he could from Camille and Rima. He kept all the same suppliers and recipes, the spices that Camille had worked years to perfect, and learned the art of stone oven pizza.

"I learned a lot from Camille in a short amount of time, absorbing all this information he accumulated over 37 years. You can see it in the product and the quality that comes out."

He also kept all of the staff, some of whom have been working at Pizza Time for over a decade.

"I think it's good to be aware of what you're buying, what you're eating, and what you're supporting. Everyone in the Passage knows they're supporting local. We know our customers by name, and people come by just to say hi – maybe offer us a Timbit, or just to say 'good luck' before the Friday rush. I have customers, who, when they land from Vancouver or the States, they come straight here, and show me their plane tickets."

Alexandra's Pizza
(Various locations)

Dimitri Neonakis got his start at Tony's Donair, but also worked for Peter Gamoulakos at PG's, making the donair cones in the back of the shop.

"You had to beat the meat pretty hard to get the air out of it. We used to beat it in bowls and shape it into cones, and sometimes the artistic side of me used to make faces in it when I was done. I would press my fingers into it to make eyes. My boss would get mad at me," he laughed.

In 1991 he opened Alexandra's Pizza. (Alexandra is his first-born daughter, while the girl on the logo is a portrait of his second daughter, from her Grade 4 graduation). The original Queen Street location was an iconic Halifax pizza shop, especially popular with students, for three decades, before closing in 2020. Dimitri claims that it was one of the first places to offer poutine in the city.

There remain 11 Alexandra's throughout the Halifax region, Charlottetown and the Cape Breton Regional Municipality.

At one point, there was even a shop in Toronto.

Alexandra's donairs are the only donair I know of in Halifax still made with lamb (40 per cent). Dimitri gets the meat shipped from trusted supplier Olympia Foods, a Chicago-based producer of gyros cones.

In Memoriam: Bash Toulany's Fine Foods
Previously located: 5553 Duffus St., Halifax
Bash immigrated to Halifax in 1973 at the age of 16 and started working right away, with his brother at a store downtown. After a while he was able to open his own grocery, originally on Hollis Street before moving to Duffus Street in the north end in the mid '70s. (68)(69) His meat shop operated there for at least 30 years before he retired in 2010.

"Back when Bash was a butcher we used to get our Christmas turkey from him," says Neil MacFarlane, a born and bred north-ender.

"I would go up to him and say, 'Hey I want a turkey!' And he'd actually put the turkey into my sled, and I would take this turkey home in my sled."

Bash eventually shifted his focus toward pizza and donairs, and gradually removed the grocery aisles and butcher counter. It all started when he noticed that his customers preferred certain choice cuts, and that they wouldn't buy the poorer cuts of meat. So he started grinding up the lower quality cuts to make donair meat, which proved lucrative. (69)

His donairs were, at one point, considered by many to be the best in Halifax. At the very least, Bash was instrumental in popularizing the donair, by wholesaling donair products to local grocery stores.

"Bash used to sing and dance, and do tricks with the knife and put on a show for you, carve the meat off the thing and tell a joke – he must have done that hundreds of times, but he seemed joyous when he did it," MacFarlane says. "I guess that's why chefs are chefs and we're not just 3D printing our food; it's the human element. To me, that's the soul of donair."

Sicilian Pizza (left) and Johnny K's (right), two corners of present-day Pizza Corner.

The Legendary Pizza Corner

"It can seem like all late-night paths lead to Pizza Corner. Rock shows and retro nights, dance parties and drinking binges can all be capped off with slices of pizza large enough to fold origami-style. Long-suffering (and doubtlessly philosophical) cashiers still spend their nights handing donair sauce over counters like nurses with pill cups filled with prescriptive cure-alls. It's the storm before the calm."
- *Melissa Buote*, The Coast (70)

The original four corners of Blowers and Grafton streets

European Food Shop: Opened in 1987 by Nick Giannopoulos (and/with/or John Kamoulakos, who owns the building) and is said to be the first spot on the corner selling slices and donairs.

Sicilian Pizza: Tarek Kostek opened the first Sicilian Pizza (on Dutch Village Road) in 1982, but the late Talat Nahas (brother of Sam and Elias, of KOD and Mezza) bought the restaurant chain in the mid-80s, and it is operated today by his sons, Mark and Joe Nahas. The Pizza Corner location was opened in the late-80s. The original Sicilian Pizza building was more than 100 years old. Despite being nominated for heritage status, it was torn down in the late-90s, and replaced by the current patio-topped Sicilian Pizza. (71)

King of Donair: Opened in the late-80s by Nick Garonis, and famous for its late-night dance parties. It closed in 2012. A lesser known fact is that at some point in the '90s there were actually two locations of King of Donair on Pizza Corner. The secondary location was on Blowers Street.

The Church: St. David's Presbyterian Church.

Left: the old Sicilian Pizza building. Right: Sicilian Pizza is torn down in the late '90s. European Food Shop is across the street.

In the late '80s this corner was transformed into what would become "Pizza Corner".

It was where party goers congregated after a night of drinking, for slices of pizza and dripping donairs. Customers would either take their food to eat on the low stone and concrete wall that bordered the church property at the sidewalk, or take their chances in the chaotic pizza shops. King of Donair was known to play club music, and allowed customers to dance on the tables.

Famously, when the G7 Summit was held in Halifax in 1995, several world leaders made a point of visiting Pizza Corner and buying donairs, proving to the world that you can't visit Halifax without making the pilgrimage. (70)

But Pizza Corner is more than just a place to eat donairs and pizza. In fact, it's far from being the best place to look for said items. The magic of Pizza Corner is the energy, the danger, the ritual.

If you were a fly on the wall on a Saturday night, you'd see booming bass gently nudging tinted windows, and ordered chaos queuing for something locals call "street meat" (it's actually Rocky's Filipino BBQ). You'd see fisticuffs and feisty drunks stuffed into paddy wagons.

On a good night you might witness a joyous group of students spontaneously break out into Barrett's Privateers. Or a dancing cop. Or a skateboarder "surfing" a water main break. Or a man stumbling about, dressed as a Christmas tree, adorned with lights and a pizza slice.

On bad nights, darker things have happened. On June 13, 1995, a 20-person "rumble" resulted in smashed windows and "blood running down the hill". In 2002, a local business owner was attacked by a group who bashed his head with a cinderblock. (71)

Extra Sauce

Pizza Corner sits on top of a 200-year-old graveyard. Saint Mary's University archaeologist Dr. Jonathan Fowler has been mapping the area he refers to as "The Halifax Necropolis" where there are about 20,000 people buried. (84)

Police respond to a fight on Pizza Corner (Photo: Julien Caesar)

By 2000, the corner was also garnering a reputation for its overflowing trash bins and litter: paper plates, discarded crusts and snacking urban birds overwhelmed the intersection. It even became an election issue that some people think caused Mayor Walter Fitzgerald to lose re-election to Peter Kelly. (71)

King of Donair eventually closed its doors in 2012. The owner Sam Nahas sued the landlord for repair costs: $25,000 for floor joists and plumbing. The building owner responded by not renewing the lease. (72)

The iconic King of Donair was replaced by a frozen yogurt shop, inciting some to declare "the death of Pizza Corner!" This was worsened when European Food Shop closed in 2015 and was replaced by Johnny K's Authentic Donairs, which broke tradition by not serving pizza.

When the fro-yo shop closed in 2017 (because, evidently, nobody wants frozen dairy after they've been drinking all night), Pizza Girls took the third corner, reinstating at least two corners of pizza and three corners of donair on the beloved intersection.

Nowadays, trash and violence are on the decline, and Pizza Corner is a cheery local landmark (even if it's still a little messy at 3 a.m.). In 2018, Sicilian Pizza erected a faux "Pizza Corner" street sign. City Hall, the bringers of fun that they are, declared that the sign was "unsanctioned", potentially confusing, and ordered it to be taken down. (73)

It's still there.

Donair from Elmsdale Pizzeria.

Elmsdale Pizza was operated by Abe and Sally Khoury for 30 years or so, but now has new ownership (essentially, Bailey's Meats – a longtime producer of donair cones).

"I went as natural as I could… no fillers, no bread crumbs," says owner Mike Klayme, of his donair meat. I nodded my approval, chowing down on one of his expertly made donairs.

Corridor Donair Trail:
Papa K's
2862 Nova Scotia Trunk 2, Shubenacadie
272 Hwy 2, Enfield, N.S (aka Enfield Pizza)

Elmsdale Pizzeria
589 Nova Scotia Trunk 2, Elmsdale

Daddy Greens
1147 Hwy 2, Lantz

Shubie Pizza
2862 Main St. W, Shubenacadie

Frank's Pizza
301 George St. Ext, Stewiacke

Jake's Pizza
72 NS-289, Brookfield

Damascus Pizzeria
239 Queen St., Truro
When the Rafih family immigrated to Canada, they started out in Calgary, but in 1974 they moved to Truro. Mahmoud "Papa" Rafih opened Damascus Donair several years later. It would stay in the family for 34 years, passed down to his sons Zack and Mahrbe, (74) but they sold it in 2002. It is now owned by Bassam Hanna.

Sadly, Bassam was forced to close the doors in 2016, as the land and building were purchased by the Nova Scotia Department of Transportation and Infrastructure Renewal, and scheduled for demolition. (75)

Bassam found a new site for Damascus in 2018, and reopened on the corner of Mill and Queen streets. He told Saltwire: "This name means a lot in Truro. A lot of generations grew up on this name. I'll be glad to see them again, I will do my best to cook them good food." (76)

Atlantic Canada
While Halifax is the home of donair, you will find donairs all over Atlantic Canada in virtually every pizza shop.

Regular Donair from Acropole

A donair from Greco Pizza.

Acropole Pizza

80 Provost St., New Glasgow, N.S.

Acropole is most known for its Pictou County-style pizza, with its spicy brown sauce and Brothers pepperoni, but their donairs are also worthy of mention. They use house-baked, thick (Greek-style) pitas, and Original Mr. Donair brand meat. A popular variation in Pictou County is the Super Donair, which adds mozzarella cheese and pepperoni to the mix.

Greco Pizza

311 Acadie Ave., Dieppe, N.B.
(and other locations across Atlantic Canada and Ontario)

Greco is a fixture in Atlantic Canada, but especially in New Brunswick, where it opened in 1977. It all started when Leander Bourque wanted to introduce the donair to New Brunswick, and got the crew from Tony's, in Halifax, to show him how to make donairs and run the business. He sold Greco to experienced franchisee, Bill Hay, in 1981, and that's when Greco really took off. It is now the largest pizza chain in Atlantic Canada, and many a homesick New Brunswicker will head straight to the nearest Greco when visiting family on holiday.

Jack's Pizza

330 University Ave, Charlottetown, P.E.I.
The island favourite.

Jaco's Restaurant

231 Churchill Blvd., Saint John, N.B.

Jaco Khoury (formerly of Shubie Pizza) had been retired from the pizza business for seven years, but once his kids had grown up and gone to university, Jaco had a bit of empty nest syndrome. Tired of sitting home doing nothing, he decided to open another donair shop. He discovered a little corner in Saint John that looked ripe for donair selling. In 2015, he opened Jaco's. The "donair warrior" was back!

Jaco's donair.

Jaco decided to make a deal with Bonté Foods, and they agreed to work with him, making his own Jaco's brand specialty donair meat. He boasts that it's gluten-free, halal and amazing.

Louis Gee's

70 West St., Corner Brook, N.L.
94 Elizabeth Dr., Gander, N.L.

"Louis Gee's makes the absolute best (east coast style) donair. Those guys have been pumping out the best donairs for years. I remember as a kid, we would sometimes get one as a treat and the largest size donair would feed the four of us and we'd have meat leftover. Now it's like a staple place to go to after the pubs/bars have closed. They're open late. REAL late. And post-pub donairs are the best." – speckle77 via Reddit

Quebec

If you ask for a donair in Quebec you might as well be speaking another language! Montreal is rich in shawarma, shish-taouk and souvlaki (they even have doner kebabs) but an utter wasteland for donairs. As I scanned the internet, I came across a post requesting help:

"Went to see a Habs game a couple years ago and I went on a search for donairs. I asked a stripper, a bouncer, 3 bartenders, and 2 cops. No one had a clue."

Il n'y a pas de donairs ici.

With one exception: it turns out there is a "secret" place to get donairs in Montreal.

En Couleur Crêpes Européennes + Donairs d'Halifax

1212 Boul de Maisonneuve Est., Montreal
En Couleur is a crêperie that happens also to specialize in Maritime fare. They serve Donairs Halifax and Greek Style Donair, both with a side of fries. The latter is served with tzatziki sauce whereas the former, I'm assured, is the real deal. They also serve garlic fingers.

Donair from En Couleur (Facebook)

"The underlying logic is that we try to serve food that is authentic," owner Yuri Airapetian tells me.

He says people are either crazy about the donair, or entirely indifferent. "Whoever walks in for a donair, they know what to expect."

So how did this unlikely marriage of cuisines come to be? It all started with Todd Langseth, a Maritimer whose family had owned a donair shop for decades. He originally opened Donair Cité, using his father's family recipe, but due to various circumstances had to shut down.

Yuri tells me that his food was good, and he hired him on as a cook at his crêpe shop. The donair eventually made its way onto the menu. While Todd has moved on to other things, En Couleur has kept his recipes, even making their own donair meat in-house. Yes, they do serve a donair crêpe.

Ontario
Ontario shares a lot of its border with the Midwestern states, and the gyro has trickled up and over to be the choice pita kebab. In cities like Windsor and London, the gyro and souvlaki reign supreme, whereas Ottawa is known for shawarma. Toronto is so multicultural you'll find just about everything represented: except the donair. In Toronto, donair shops open and close, and occasionally there are impostors that incite Twitter riots.

"The last time I tried a donair in Ontario I received what I can only assume was strips of rubber boots seasoned with Montreal steak spice. Every city outside of Hali has 'that one place' that makes them authentically, but it'd probably be better to make your own." – KingSulley (from Reddit).

Ottawa: Shawarma Town
When I asked my blogging associate, Murray Wong (Eat This Town Ottawa), for a soundbite about Ottawa donairs, he just sent me a GIF of a dumpster fire.

"The worst offenders are often pizza/shawarma places; they typically aren't trying to emulate the Halifax donair, but rather the word is used in the place of the traditional 'doner' or as a catch-all for the various forms of spiced beef cooked on a vertical grill," he says.

The Ottawa donair scene is actually a shawarma scene, with mostly bad-faith attempts to cater to Maritimers. I've chosen to feature two Ottawa donair shops, in order to portray the different approaches to the dish.

Centretown Donair (From Murray Wong at Eat This Town: Ottawa)

Centretown Donair & Pizza
422 Bronson Ave., Ottawa

Gus Anbara opened his East Coast pizza shop in Ottawa's Centretown district in 2008. He has made quite a name for himself, serving the best donairs in Ottawa, keeping true to the Halifax tradition. In fact, some say his donairs are on par with the very best of Halifax.

"I was always proud of my donairs even when I was in Halifax, but that's what everyone says," he told me.

He arrived from Lebanon in 1984, settled in Cole Harbour, and learned the art of donair at Tripoli Pizza (now closed) on Portland Street. He also ran Nova Pizza (on the No. 7 Highway) and Paolo's Pasta House with his brother. He moved to Ottawa in 1992.

He makes his donairs the traditional way, even making his own donair meat.

"You have to do it yourself, or else you're just like everyone else. If you're watching the Food Network, and 10 different people write down the same recipe exactly, you'll have 10 different versions. Food comes from the heart."

In a 2011 CTV News Best of Ottawa viewers poll for Best Shawarma, Centretown Donair (which doesn't serve shawarma) somehow secured the No. 2 spot.

"The customers voted me in!" laughs Gus. This must be some good donair if voters were able to hijack the vote in a shawarma city in favour of a Halifax donair shop!

Romeo Donair & Pizza

1580 Merivale Rd, Nepean

Murray Wong writes: "Romeo's large, back-lit menu board above the counter gives centre stage to their donair. It even goes so far as to describe its Turkish origins, as well as the ingredients. So, while it's decidedly non-Haligonian, they're obviously committed to what they do. The spit of meat that was slowly rotating behind the counter eased my fears of grey, pre-cut slices."

For a staunch Halifax purist, I was surprised to see that he found it "quite enjoyable," even with its sweet and bitter tahini sauce and crunchy lettuce (they do offer a sweet and sour sauce as well).

Romeo's Donair has been around for decades, and offers an old school alternative to the new wave of Maritime-themed restaurants.

Romeo Donair (From Murray Wong at Eat This Town: Ottawa)

Toronto: Centre of the Universe (but not donairs)
Collage Falafel

450 Ossington Ave., Toronto

Owners Bardhyl and Oljana Musa met in Albania, where Oljana was a chef and Bardhyl was head of food and beverage for the district. In 1998, they immigrated to Canada, and in 2002 they bought College Falafel. They kept the name but started serving Albanian specialties alongside the usual falafel and shawarma. (77)

College Falafel.

When I paid a visit in 2015, I was told that College Falafel was the first to sell Halifax donairs in Toronto. Oljana told me that a guy from D'Escousse, Cape Breton had come into their shop in 2004, and encouraged them to tap into the East Coast market.

The mysterious man was Brad Delorey, and I got in touch with him to hear his side of the story.

"If I remember correctly, the owners were already serving 'donairs,'" he says. "But the donairs they were serving were borderline healthy and I was like, 'that's not a donair.' I told them a donair is pita, meat, onion, tomato and sauce. ... It's messy, it's unhealthy and it's delicious.

"My mother, who lives in Isle Madame, Nova Scotia, owned a pizza and donair shop at the time so I contacted her and she happily provided her recipe for the all-important donair sauce."

It is not the most authentic donair; the meat is chopped up and the wrap is prepared like a stuffed pita. They'll add tabouleh if you want.

"I was not transported to Pizza Corner," Brad admitted.

But College Falafel proudly advertises "East Coast Donairs" on their awning. A rare sight in downtown Toronto.

Jessy's Pizza
2200 Dundas St. W, Toronto
This Halifax-based chain now has a location in Toronto, making it the most authentic Halifax-style pizza shop in Toronto proper.

East Coast Donair & Grill
664 Bloor St. W, Toronto
Evelyn A. writes on Yelp:
"Alright, alright, alright. Everyone calm down. I grew up in Nova Scotia, and I'm here to set a few things straight.

Tonight I was desperate for something comforting, found this place on UberEats, and boom goes the dynamite:

If you're after a euro doner or gyro, and aren't after a proper East Coast donair, then this might not be for you. However, if you know what an East Coast donair is, and are nostalgic for that sweet sticky sauce coating spicy beef with onions and tomatoes, ooooh doggy, you'll be thrilled!"

In Memoriam: The Fuzz Box

Previously Located: 1246 Danforth Ave., Toronto
The Fuzz Box existed from 2012 to 2017. Neil Hohn hails from Berwick, Nova Scotia, and it was his dream to open a donair shop, despite never having worked in one. He made 12 attempts before perfecting his recipe; roasting his meat in loaves, rather than using a vertical rotisserie. As he was located on The Danforth, which is known for its Greek food, he inadvertently ordered pita bread from a Greek bakery, not realizing that it would be different from the Arabic pitas of Halifax. It was a blessing in disguise, for Neil realized that Greek pitas were more sturdy and pliable, if not exactly Halifax-style. The Fuzz Box is certainly missed.

The Fuzz Box.

401 Highway Donair Trail

Highway 401 connects the Quebec/Ontario border to the Canada/U.S. border via Windsor. Along this route are various cities, each with their own donair shop in tribute to the Halifax donair.

Halifax Original Donair

295 Main St. E, Milton
3300 Fairview St., Burlington
Halifax Original Donair opened in 2008 in Milton, and continues to be the best donair in the GTA, made in the old school way.

"We chose a name that reflects what we're offering people: true authentic Halifax-style donair from the '80s," says co-owner Troy Power, who learned the art of donair under the legendary Nick Garonis, second owner of King of Donair.

"It was incredible. You're talking about the guy who basically took the King of Donair name and put it on the map!"

Troy opened Halifax Original Donair with his best friend, Jimmy Tsouros, who is the son of a traditional Greek donair family (his father opened Fairview Pizza in the 1970s). Troy and Jimmy met in high school, and they worked the early '90s donair circuit together, from Fairview to Pizza Corner.

A donair from Halifax Donair in Milton.

Eventually, they left Nova Scotia for greener pastures, which in this case meant Ontario. It was here that they would meet their wives: Jimmy met Tina, and Troy fell for Tina's sister, Nancy. The couples married and settled in Milton. This is where they fulfilled their dream of opening a donair shop together. Then in 2010, they opened a second location in Burlington. Now, Jimmy and Tina are in charge of the Milton shop, while Troy and Nancy run the Burlington shop.

In addition to authentic, Halifax-style donairs, they sell donair salads, subs, nachos, poutines and plates.

House of Donair (formerly Famous King)
505 Princess St., Kingston
394 Princess St., Kingston
Rumoured to have once been a King of Donair, the current owner informs me that they haven't changed the recipe since the original owner brought it from Halifax.

Nova Deli
200 N Front St., Belleville

Down East Donairs
23 Bond St. E, Oshawa
Opened in 2011 by Shane and Christina Walker. They never set out to be restaurant owners. Shane has a background as an iron worker and Christina worked for the government. But a lack of authentic donair in Durham inspired them to take matters into their own hands. (78)

Sammy's Donair
453 Guelph Line, Burlington

Stobie's Pizza
484 Richmond St., London
Opened in 1997 by Bernie, John & Carol Stobie, transplants from Lower Sackville, N.S., who simply told me: "We knew we wanted donairs on the menu, so they were." Not only do they sell authentic East Coast donair, but they do garlic fingers as well.

The Prairies
The donair arrived in Edmonton in the early '80s and has since become the street food par excellence in the City of Champions. The Edmonton donair has its own established tradition, and there are more shops than I could ever hope to feature. As for the rest of the Prairie provinces, well, it varies. Northern Alberta has a different donair scene than southern Alberta, which probably has something to do with the East Coast population in the respective regions. The donair has trickled into Saskatchewan, but hasn't really caught on in Manitoba.

With that said…

Best Pizza & Donair
1469 Pembina Hwy, Winnipeg
"The donair I had at Best Pizza & Donair came closest to my Istanbul ideal. For one reason, because (according to the server) it's made in Turkish fashion; for another, because it is made from scratch with fresh meats," writes Marion Warhaft in the Winnipeg *Free Press*. (79)

Meanwhile, Linda H. writes on Trip Advisor: "We haven't found a great donair since living in Halifax, NS, and this donair was superb!"

It would seem that Best Pizza & Donair offers the best of both worlds, to a city that isn't exactly known for its donairs.

Prairie Donair
4115 Rochdale Blvd., Regina
4B 701 Robert St., Swift Current, Sask.
2410 Division Ave., Medicine Hat, Alta.
Joshua Bagchi grew up in Regina, and food always played a central role in his family. According to the Prairie Donair website, "We would start planning supper right after we finish our breakfast. True story. Our mom's homemade meals were to die for. That's why we set out to build a restaurant with a homemade feel serving our customers food that we loved."

A donair from Prairie Donair (From Facebook).

Joshua opened his first Prairie Donair restaurant in 2010 on Regina's Quance Street. He had to borrow $40,000 to make it happen, but he quickly learned the ropes and the business became successful. He opened a second location on Dewdney Avenue in 2016. Since then he has opened three more locations in Regina, one in Emerald Park (just outside Regina) and locations in Swift Current, Medicine Hat, Moose Jaw, Yorkton and Prince Albert.

Inspired by the fast food franchise model, Joshua has introduced the first donair franchise to Saskatchewan and plans to take it nationwide. He has his sights on Calgary and Winnipeg, but has also had franchise inquiries from Ontario, Quebec and even New Brunswick. (80)

Prairie Donair offers 22 types of veggies and 21 types of sauces, but also pays tribute to the East Coast donair, with the "famous donair sweet sauce". Not only that, they make a Canadian maple donair with maple chili sauce. My interest is piqued! But the signature dish is:

The Spicy PD Signature: donair meat grilled with onions and jalapeños, drizzled with honey garlic, and topped with lettuce, banana peppers, mozza and buffalo sauce.

Liberty Donair
3702 Kepler St., Whitecourt, Alta.

Cleopatra's Donair & Pita
12-7110 50 Ave, Red Deer, Alta.

Blowers & Grafton
709 Edmonton Trail NE, Calgary
10550 82 Ave. NW, Edmonton
"When I first started eating donairs as a kid, coming back from hockey practice with my dad and my coach in Bedford, my donair place was the original Martha's in Bedford. I still remember exactly how that tasted. That was my introduction," says Josh Robinson.

Today, Josh is the brainchild behind Blowers & Grafton, a Pizza Corner-themed restaurant, serving craft beer and cocktails, with locations in both Calgary and Edmonton. I had a long Nova Scotian chat with Josh, learning all about his entrepreneurial journey.

Blowers & Grafton (Facebook)

When Josh was 17, he had a cotton candy stand on the Halifax waterfront boardwalk, in a colourful little shed his father helped him build.

Donair from Uncle Moe's (Facebook)

At the time, there was only a seafood shack and a Beavertails catering to hungry tourists, who would always ask Josh where they could find a donair. So Josh got permission from the Waterfront Corp. to open a bigger kiosk, and Waterfront Pizza & Wraps was born. He brought donairs to the Halifax Waterfront, where today you will find everything from poutine to tofu bowls.

Josh moved to Calgary in 2013, and eventually landed an oil and gas job downtown, but he says he was always an entrepreneur at heart.

"The seed was planted almost immediately when I came to Calgary. The first weekend I remember being with some buddies from Halifax. I tried to order a pepperoni pizza and some garlic fingers, and the guy on the phone was like – what's garlic fingers?"

When oil plummeted, as it tends to do, Josh was laid off with severance pay and decided to open a place with his favourites from Pizza Corner and the Halifax Waterfront: donairs, clams, lobster rolls.

"What if I had Alexander Keith's in the fridge?" he thought.

In 2017, Josh opened Blowers & Grafton on Calgary's Edmonton Trail. There were kitchen parties, craft taps and a menu that will please the most discriminating Maritimer and hesitant Calgarian alike. At first, he made his own donair meat from scratch, but when he realized how much extra work that is, he outsourced to a local producer.

"I was happy with the flavour, but it wasn't juicy enough," he said. So now he gets his meat shipped from Mr. Donair.

"I've been obsessed with food my whole life," he says. "So everything has to be as good as we can possibly make it."

Scotian Style
5268 Marlborough Dr. NE, Calgary
Scotian Style was opened in 2016 in Calgary's Marlborough neighbourhood, and had everything you could possibly ask for in a Halifax-style pizza shop (including seafood). They even made keto donairs with a 100% cheese "pita".

Scotian Style has recently announced that they are converting their Marlborough Drive shop to an East Coast specialty market with fresh seafood and "back home" items. While the future of Scotian Style remains unclear, they say that they may continue to do a fish and chips and donair take-out counter, and there is also talk of a mobile take-out trailer.

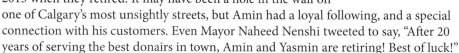

A keto donair from Scotian Style (from Facebook)

In Memoriam: Amin Donairs
Previously located: 163-328 Center St. SE, Calgary
Opened in 1994 by Amin and his wife, Yasmin, and closed in 2013 when they retired. It may have been a hole in the wall on one of Calgary's most unsightly streets, but Amin had a loyal following, and a special connection with his customers. Even Mayor Naheed Nenshi tweeted to say, "After 20 years of serving the best donairs in town, Amin and Yasmin are retiring! Best of luck!"

A family member told me that "Amin doesn't make donairs much anymore, but when he does, they are still as good as they have always been."

Amin's shop on 7th Ave SE.

The Edmonton Scene:

Queen Donair
10068 156 St. NW, Edmonton
10752 Jasper Ave., Edmonton
12914 50 St. NW, Edmonton

Marco's Famous
10371 112 St. NW, Edmonton

Homestyle Donair
3424 43 Ave. NW, Edmonton

Swiss Donair
8308 144 Ave. NW, Edmonton
Wajdi Chehimi was born in Lebanon in 1984, but was also a Canadian citizen through his father (who had been a Canadian citizen since 1974). When Wajdi was only four years old, the family immigrated to Canada at the tail end of the Lebanese Civil War. He grew up in the Dickinsfield neighbourhood of Edmonton, and he is still there today, now the proud owner of Swiss Donair.

Wajdi has been working in the donair industry since he was 14, working in his father's donair shop in south Edmonton before getting into the business for himself. At 19, he bought Swiss Donair (with a loan from the bank and a co-signer). At first there were only two employees: Wajdi and his mom. Nine months later, his father sold his donair shop and joined the family at Swiss Donair. That was around 2004. Nowadays, Swiss Donair employs 25 people.

Swiss Donair.

Swiss Donair has a fast-food format, with donairs sold in combos with fries and pop. It is a bustling spot, and Wajdi has it running like a well oiled machine. His Dad apparently pioneered the use of the donair bag, which provides an extra level of defence against drippings. When I visited Swiss Donair in 2016, I was impressed by how clean and efficient it was, with donairs wrapped expertly tight in true Edmonton fashion, and spot on flavours, for this Haligonian.

"I'm 35 years old now, have been in the restaurant/donair business for 20 years, believe it or not," Wajdi Chehimi says. "This is all I know, cooking, dealing with people, innovating. We have taken Swiss Donair from a no name to a brand name and a staple of Edmonton hot spots to eat donairs."

Top Donair
8210 144 Ave. NW, Edmonton
10084 Jasper Ave., Edmonton
8210 144 Ave. NW, Edmonton

Jumbo Donair
4220 66 St. NW, Edmonton

Eddie's Donair
16767 91 St. NW, Edmonton

PrimeTime Donair
6572 28 Ave. NW, Edmonton
3928 17 St. NW, Edmonton
16529 50 St. NW #101, Edmonton
11343 104 Ave. NW, Edmonton

Donairs from PrimeTime in Edmonton.

PrimeTime is known for their PrimeTime Special Donairs, where they toss your donair meat with your choice of flavour (bold BBQ, sweet & spicy, honey garlic, butter chicken, spicy fire or pineapple curry – whoa) and sauté it with green peppers, onions and mushrooms. It is then topped off with your choice of donair sauce and fresh veggies.

Simon King Donair
9070 51 Ave. NW, Edmonton

Amean Donair
3450 99 St. NW, Edmonton

Richard's Donair
12648 137 Ave. NW, Edmonton

Simply Donairs
140 St. Albert Trail Unit 245, St. Albert
9004 50 St. NW, Edmonton

Donair Stop
9718 Ottewell Rd. NW, Edmonton

High Voltage
10387 63 Ave. NW, Edmonton
High Voltage is Edmonton's "fancy" donair. Fluffy, sea-salted pitas are

An East Coast Donair at High Voltage.

grilled with donair meat and a sweet donair sauce spiked with vanilla. There are also varieties such as Greek, Caribbean jerk and blue cheese. It is unlike any donair you'll ever have, making some critics question whether it qualifies as a donair at all. But its legions of fans say it is the best donair in Edmonton, bar none. You will just have to go try it for yourself!

Donairs from Supreme (Facebook)

Mom's Donair
16209 Stony Plain Rd, Edmonton

The Northern Trail

Supreme Pizza
Moe Akkad opened Supreme Pizza in 2011, but he gives credit to Elmer Mockler for his success.

When he first opened, he didn't know anything about the industry.

"It just happened that I got into the pizza business. But I didn't know about pizza whatsoever, I just got into the market at a good time," he says.

He admits his product wasn't very good when he first opened. He had doughy pizza and mass-produced donair cones from a Maritime wholesaler.

So he called up his friend, Geoff Mockler, whose father had opened one of the very first pizzerias in Atlantic Canada: Elmer's Pizza. Geoff flew up from New Brunswick and stayed with him for six weeks, teaching him the art of pizza and donair. Elmer Mockler died in 2017 at 77 years old, but his recipes live on at Supreme Pizza.

"Everything from my donair sauce to my pizza dough, is his recipes."

Moe started reading pizza literature and attending conferences like the Vegas Pizza Expo. He makes his own pita bread with the same dough he uses for his pizza. It involves a meticulous proofing process in which it must rest for 36 hours.

Whereas a lot of Alberta pizza shops use mayonnaise as the base for their sweet sauce, Moe calls this sacrilegious.

"It's like someone came here and told everyone how to do things wrong."

If a customer walks in and asks for sweet sauce, Moe tells them, "We don't have sweet sauce here. We have donair sauce.

"I know it sounds cheesy, but I love the pizza business. My wife gets tired of my crust ideologies. She's a psychologist. She sits and listens."

I talked to Moe during the coronavirus outbreak, and since then Supreme Pizza has sadly closed its doors. He had already suffered through the 2016 Fort McMurray wildfire, and 2020 brought the coronavirus pandemic and, finally, the Fort McMurray flooding disaster which broke the camel's back.

Moe says he will definitely reopen in a new location in Fort Mac as soon as the time is right.

PK's Corner
101 Riverstone Ridge, Fort McMurray
You wouldn't expect much from a donair at a takeout counter tucked away in a Petro Canada, but PK's Corner won the title of Best Donair in Your McMurray Magazine in 2019.

Opened by the Kalogirou family in the fall of 2010, it started out as a convenience store with a tiny take-away counter, but grew to offer a full menu of pizza, pasta and fried chicken. They even have garlic fingers! The donairs come with lettuce, onion, tomato and cheese with your choice of sour cream or sweet sauce. (81)

Jomaa's Pizza
102 Millennium Dr., Fort McMurray
8706 Franklin Ave., Fort McMurray
208 Beacon Hill Dr., Fort McMurray
101 Signal Rd., Fort McMurray
The Beacon Hill location opened in 1990, and Jomaa's has been a beloved institution ever since. In 2020 they expanded to Edmonton, opening a shop on 127th St. NW.

Hu's Pizza & Donairs
10020 Franklin Ave., Fort McMurray
Opened by a Cape Bretoner, who sticks to the Scotian script.

Cosmos Pizza & Donair
700 Signal Rd. #9, Fort McMurray
9713 Hardin St., Fort McMurray
I stumbled upon an old Facebook fan page for Cosmos, which was created because "I couldn't allow those yuppies from Jomaas to have their own group and not us!"

Fort Mac definitely has a cult following for each of its donair shops, with passionate rhetoric and ritualistic consumption.

I reached out to one of the Cosmos disciples, Allan Millisic, who told me: "People that know their donairs will not get the strip of processed cheese that places put on, but will ask for 'real mozzarella', the same shredded cheese they put on pizzas. And it can either be melted with a quick turn through the oven or not. Some people like myself get creative. I enjoy hot banana peppers and BBQ sauce on mine from time to time."

Owner Ali Samfadi gets his meat shipped from New Brunswick's Bonté Foods, and makes a zippy donair sauce with a special ingredient: Miracle Whip! (82)

British Columbia
On the West Coast, the word "donair" is used as a synonym for döner kebab in its most generic sense. They tend to be stuffed pitas and "grilled pita donairs", with any range of fillings. While many shops advertise a "Halifax-style", they never seem to be true to form. British Columbia is more of a health-conscious province than Nova Scotia, and many shops have more of a fresh and healthy take on donairs.

North City Donair
415 George St., Prince George
Marc-André Chartrand is a poutine-loving French Canadian lumberjack from Vancouver Island, who wanted to bring his two favourite Canadian comfort foods to the northern city of Prince George: donair and poutine. In 2017, he opened North City Donair.

Marc-André was born and raised in Victoria, where The Donair Shop was an iconic restaurant when he was growing up, along the Esquimalt Road. The other restaurant that imprinted itself upon his childhood was La Belle Patate. Marc-André also spent many years working (and eating donairs) in Alberta, so when he moved to Prince George, it didn't make sense to him that there was no donair shop.

"Am I the only one that loves them so much?" he asked himself, and "Why does nobody know how to make a proper Quebec poutine?"

North City Donair (from Facebook)

Donair Dude's Davie St. shop (from Facebook)

He says his inspiration came from Liberty Donair, his favourite donair shop, in Whitecourt, Alberta.

"He (the owner) inspired me because he got out of the oil patch and opened a donair shop. I got out of hand falling, logging and chainsaw work. Freedom from camp jobs. Allows me to be home finally. Donairs = Freedom Wrap," he concluded our conversation.

North City Donair has a rampant lion and fleur-de-lis right on their website, representing the Nova Scotian and Quebecois themes of the menu, which is divided into two main sections: poutine and donairs. The T-Rex Donair combines all worlds, with chicken, donair meat, Montreal smoked meat, bacon, mozzarella cheese, tomato and onion with your choice of sweet donair sauce, tzatziki, garlic sauce or hummus.

Athena Donair
3945A Quadra St., Victoria
Athena Donair is known for its Foot Long Donair in homemade pita bread. The menu says it comes with a side of tzatziki sauce, but I've heard that it's more of a "sweet Halifax style tzatziki", whatever that means!

In Memoriam: The Donair Shop
Previously Located: 1243 Esquimalt Rd., Victoria
The Donair Shop was a fixture on the Esquimalt Road for 30 years, run by the Dunahee family. It was sold in 2017, and shortly afterwards the township purchased the land and demolished the building.

The new owner was looking for a new place to open up shop as recently as 2018 but so far… nothing. The collective fingers of donair lovers everywhere are crossed that one day there will be a return. (83)

Davie Street Donair Tour
There are a lot of donair shops along Vancouver's Davie Street, and you could probably get a good sense of the offerings if you walked from Granville Street to English Bay Beach. It's a nice walk and a great way to get a taste of Vancouver!

Donair Dude
1172 Davie St., Vancouver
Donair Dude was opened by two friends, Savas Gorgun and Tibet Arikan, who had both come to Canada for university and met while studying engineering. One day they were walking along Davie Street and they thought, "We should open our own donair shop."

They opened Donair Dude on Davie Street just in time for the 2010 Winter Olympics. They worked 45 days straight, living in the apartment connected to the back of the shop, and reinvested their money back into the company.

They now have eight locations, a third partner (Abdul), and their own production facility. Donair Dude is known for their grilled donairs, stuffed to the brim with fresh and tasty ingredients.

"We are from Turkey and we grew up with donair culture," Tibet tells me. "It is our national dining/fast food product. I personally didn't know about Halifax sauce. I learned it here and I love it. You can't find Halifax sauce in Turkey nor in Europe. I believe this is what makes donair unique. It is a very versatile food that can be adapted and modified easily.

Mr. Greek Donair Town
1173 Granville St., Vancouver

Donair King
1028 Davie St., Vancouver

Best Bite Donair
1091 Davie St., Vancouver

Donair Spot
1179 Denman St,, Vancouver

The North
The territories are the last place I would think to look for a donair, but I was curious: has the donair made its way up past the 60th parallel? It turns out that even Iqaluit has two restaurants serving donairs. It just goes to show how far and wide the donair has really travelled!

Big Bear's Donair Del Diablo with jalapenos and hot sauce (Facebook)

Big Bear Donair
4161 4 Ave. #11, Whitehorse
Travis Milos was introduced to the donair while living in B.C. (he thinks he had his first one in the unlikely locale of Kelowna) and realized that nobody in Whitehorse was making them.

He and his wife already owned a couple of pubs in Whitehorse, so they thought donairs would be a fun business to add to their repertoire. Travis ate a whole bunch of donairs in Vancouver and Edmonton, to get a feel for what's out there, and he figured out the recipes by looking online.

"We just winged it and did our own thing," he told me. "We have an East Coaster donair, and people come here and say it's closer than anything in Vancouver."

At first, they made their own donair cones, but Travis quickly realized that nobody actually does this anymore. It's too much work! But they do occasionally make Yukon-raised elk donairs, when it's in season.

Big Bear has an Edmonton-style donair (The Classic), a Halifax-style donair (The East Coaster) and plenty of customizations because, "to each their own." Travis says that he's eaten so many "research donairs" that he's now sick of them, and his favourite thing on the menu is the Suicide Shawarma.

You can enjoy it all on Big Bear's sunny patio, with a nice selection of craft beer, spirits and wine.

Yummy Shawarma
1089 Mivvik St., Iqaluit
Yummy Shawarma serves a donair with your choice of garlic, hummus or tahini sauce (so bring your own sweet sauce).

Main Street
5012 53 St., Yellowknife
4905 Franklin Ave., Yellowknife

Zillman's Grill
2193 2nd Ave, Whitehorse

Opened in June 2019 by cook/owner Al Alrawashdeh who worked in Halifax-area donair shops before relocating to the Yukon. He has always had a soft spot for East Coast donairs and that delicious sweet sauce.

8

Toilet Reading

It would seem that just about everyone has a donair story – some encounter with the dripping demon that has led to madness, sickness, romance, camaraderie, nostalgia or, at the very least, a well-earned shower.

The idea to collect donair stories actually came from Leo Salloum at Tony's Pizza, who wanted to make an archive of these anecdotes. I thought that these tales would make for some good, er, bathroom reading, so I put out the call and I was showered with your saucy submissions.

Many of you have a donair to thank for sending you into labour, or getting you through a hard time. And a disturbing number of you have stories involving the reckless pairing of donairs with chocolate milk!

The donair has, perhaps, been unfairly stigmatized as a food that wreaks havoc on the digestive system. If we're being honest, alcohol is usually the common denominator in violent bodily mishaps. It is clear that many of you have been competing in the Donair Olympics: bigger, faster, drunker! I would argue that a regular-sized donair is a balanced lunch, fit for any office worker's post-gym recovery.

But I didn't always feel this way.

My first encounter with the donair was a noxious phantom odour that terrorized my tiny soul. I couldn't have been older than four when I went to the doctor's office and was hit by an olfactory offence that overwhelmed my vulnerable nervous system. I started sobbing, covering every sensory organ with my frantic little hands, as tears streamed down my face. The doctor sheepishly explained to my mother that he had enjoyed a donair for lunch in his office. I didn't know what a donair was, but I knew that it was evil.

My second donair memory was hearing some urban legend about a donair shop that put a "secret ingredient" in their sauce. The next thing I know, I'm at a picnic table watching my friend and her mother eating donairs. I was mesmerized and disgusted by the thick white sauce, glistening atop the mound of mysterious brown meat, while I safely ate my slice of pizza.

The truth is, I did not grow up eating donairs. My Dad was more of a seafood guy, and my mother wouldn't be caught dead with a stinkin' donair. It wasn't until I was 17 that I was initiated by my donair-obsessed boyfriend. He came from one of those "donair families" – you know, the ones who have Sunday Donair Night instead of roast beef or whatever. His mother would make a donair-spiced meatloaf, served with pita bread and all the fixings. It was fascinating to me.

He introduced me to my first donair at Charlie's Pizza, located between their Auburndale home and the Bridgewater town limits. I watched my boyfriend pound back his donair with vigor, groaning and sweating, eyes glazed over, slowly overtaken by their drooping lids, as he slumped in his chair, holding his belly, somehow sickly satisfied.

I continued to eat donairs with him as a bonding exercise, but it would be years before I started to appreciate the donair as a symbol of regional pride. Like many other Maritimers, I didn't realize what I had until I moved away.

Now, of course, I'm obviously pretty dedicated to championing the donair as a national dish. But my story had to start somewhere, and it has been a wild ride from childhood bogeyman to writing a book about it. This chapter is a collection of feats of strength, airing of grievances, epic tales, anecdotes, sociables, and love stories.

Donair Stories

I can't remember exactly how long, but within a few months of dating this girl we went out with some of my friends for a night of drinking. When we were walking back to her house at the end of the night we stopped and got a donair. When we got back to her place I smoked a joint that was probably too large for my state of inebriation at the time.

I told her I was too stoned to use my arms, so she would take a bite, then she would feed me a bite. This kept going until I passed out about halfway through the football we had purchased. I woke up the next morning on her couch with her roommate watching TV, and the stench of stale donair in my face.

That amazing woman is now my wife and we both mentioned that night in our vows. I love her.
- Steve S. (Cole Harbour, NS)

One time when I was drunk, I left an uneaten donair in a cab, so I called every cab company at 3 a.m. asking if they had found my missing donair.
Shayna MacDiarmid (Riverview, NB)

My dad used to have a restaurant back in the '70s-'90s. When I was in junior high (early '90s), for my lunches he used to deliver me a donair sandwich. It would just be donair meat on white sliced bread. Most of my junior high peers thought I was odd to eat that almost every day for lunch.
- Margreek (Halifax)

I was sitting eating a donair with a couple buddies late in the evening after a night out drinking. I notice at the table next to us, this young guy, presumably blacked out, just devouring his donair. Like most shops around here, this place serves their donairs wrapped in a light tinfoil/paper material. This guy had unwrapped the first bit of tinfoil from the donair, but presumably forgot to unwrap the second half, and continued eating the rest of the donair - tinfoil and all. He was so blacked out that he ate the entirety of the rest of the tinfoil wrap without noticing, washed it down with a sip of his drink, and walked off.
- Kelly (Edmonton, AB)

Went home for my cousin's wedding in '98. I was tasked with the Toast to the Bride, and Grammy said no drinking beforehand by any of the speech makers. Two minutes later I see Uncle Eber (the father of young cousin Kim) bellying up to the bar. Cheater, I say. So I decided to catch up as soon as I made my toast. Mind you, the reception was at the Junior Ranks' Mess, and rum was cheap as chips back then. Two bucks a shot, so a fiver gets you a double and 25% tip for the bar. Ballin'.

$100 later we were all ready to leave the old ones there, and headed to bars. JJ Rossy's, Split Crow, up to the Liquor Dome, cousin in her dress, the groom in his tux, and the rest of us dapper as dapper could be. I kinda lost everyone in the Dome and so I went on a wander. When I hit Pizza Corner, the smell of donair wafted over me and slapped enough sense into me to order a donair slice. Five years in Ontario, surrounded by gyros and tzatziki sauce, were all washed away while I was in a donair trance. When I came back to my body, I saw that the sauce did not all quite stay on the slice. Fair game, I thought. Hate suits anyhoo, and the jacket was a decent sacrifice. The bin, or the bench, I'm not sure where it went, but it didn't come back with me.
- Fred (Digby, NS)

Season, 4, Episode 8 (Workin' Man). Bubbles (Mike Smith), Ricky (Robb Wells) and Julien (John Paul Tremblay) eat at a King of Donair while hashing out a plan to ship drugs through a courier. (Photo used with permission from Trailer Park Boys Incorporated)

Donair Heroes: The Trailer Park Boys
The popular television show, *Trailer Park Boys*, features the donair in several episodes. For example, in Season 4, Episode 2, Randy prostitutes himself in front of the King of Donair for coupons while Julien decides he's going to live out back where his car broke down. Bubbles finds him "drunk on swish, dancing around with an old f'ing dirty dog, eating pizza crusts off the f'ing ground."

Then in Season 4, Episode 8, the boys are shown planning, scheming and eating donairs in the King of Donair, while people dance in the background. Every time the shop is featured on the show, there are always people dancing and swaying in the background. It seems comedic, but the King of Donair on Pizza Corner was always filled with dancing people on the weekends, so the TPB portrayal is true to form.

In 2018, he was the first to eat a six-pound donair at Alexandra's Pizza in Sydney, N.S., which he completed in 28 minutes and 30 seconds. Not to be outdone, King of Donair made Joel a 10-pound donair on National Donair Day, 2019. He finished in 42 minutes, 16 seconds.

Joel Hansen also holds the record for most donairs eaten in one sitting. On New Year's Day, 2019, he ate 19 regular donairs, weighing in at 10 pounds, in under an hour. The challenge took place at King of Donair, and cost him about $150.

When I asked him what his relationship to donairs was like outside of competitive eating, he replied, "Despite consuming countless pounds of donair in my life, they are always a delicious treat which I enjoy occasionally throughout the year."

I worked at what was then Venus Pizza from 1998-2003 on Gottingen. We sold 3 small donairs for 6 bucks and had a belly buster which was a football size. One night around 3 am a drunk mess of a dude came in from the since burned down North End Tavern. He ate an entire belly buster and passed out in a booth with his face/hair lying in the pita bread and sauce remnants, it was pretty gross. We couldn't wake him and had no interest in touching him so we called the cops who escorted him in to their vehicle for what was probably a drunk tank trip. The pizza driver that night went over to clean up the table and instead yelled, "F**k that shit I'm done for the night," cashed out and left. The dude had left the stankiest runny diarrhea all over the booth and side of the table legs. It was like he either pulled his pants half off to do it or blew a hole through his jeans.
The magic of alcohol and donairs.
- Jon (Dartmouth, NS)

I had long hair. I fell asleep on one. Went to the bathroom in the dark. Turned the light on when in front of the mirror. Nearly had a heart attack. A parasite stuck to my head!
- Jeff (Halifax, NS)

I was going to school, 20 years old and living with 2 roommates in a town house on Stairs Street, Halifax in 2005.

Had a party on Saturday. Went out to the bars, and a few people came back and we were hungry. Our buddy Chad, who was up from Pictou County for the weekend, called the pizza place (I don't remember which one). He ordered a couple pizzas and asked for 8 large donair sauce, for dipping the pizza. When the delivery man came, he brought the pizza and 8 large donair SUBS. Subs were like 12 bucks each so the whole order was around $200, and we were all pretty broke from the night out. We tried to explain, and the delivery guy was pissed. Chad somehow talked the driver into taking a lesser amount of money, and he gave the guy his new pair of sneakers as collateral until he could pay the next day, and it all worked out in the end. Me and my roommates ate donair subs for breakfast lunch and dinner for a few days.
- Adam (Halifax)

I was at a place in Whistler that had 'Halifax Donairs' on the menu. I asked if they knew what that meant. Was told 'the chef is from Halifax and makes a real Halifax donair.' I thought - let's try this and ordered one. They then asked 'chicken or beef'?

I left.
- Dale (Brantford, Ontario)

Donair Hero: Michael Dinn

Michael ("Moose") Dinn was well respected in the Halifax IT community, and also Halifamous for his antics on Halifax Twitter. He was always coming up with creative food combinations, secret menu items, and if anyone, anywhere, misrepresented his beloved donair online, he would find them and school them. With his website donair. org, he was a true connoisseur of the Canadian kebab. When he passed away in 2018, Halifax lost a donair crusader and friend to all. #teamnolettuce

One of the things that Michael was known for was getting restaurants to put together "secret menu" dishes for him. When that didn't work, he would take matters into his own hands. He once made donair lasagna and posted a step-by-step tutorial for the process on Twitter. I've done my best to recreate his recipe here.

Michael Dinn's Donair Lasagna
Ingredients:
9 lasagna noodles
1 lb sliced donair meat (from your favourite donair shop)
1 medium onion, diced
1 can diced tomatoes (drained)
3 cups cottage cheese (make sure to buy a 750 g tub)
1 egg
2 cups shredded mozza (you may want extra)
1 cup shredded parmesan, divided
1 Tbsp dried parsley
Pinch of cayenne pepper
Donair sauce (for serving)

Michael Dinn. (Dagley Media).

Instructions:
1. Heat oven to 375°F
2. Cook lasagna noodles according to package instructions.
3. Drain, and rinse with cold water. Set aside.
4. In a medium bowl, combine spices, cottage cheese, 1 cup mozzarella, ½ cup parmesan and egg.
5. In a 9 x 12 x 3-inch dish, make a layer of donair meat, onions and diced tomatoes.
6. Put one third of the cheese mixture on top, spreading out to cover the layer of meat.
7. Cover with a layer of 3 noodles.

8. Repeat the layers: meat, onions & tomatoes, cheese mixture, noodles. Drizzle this layer with donair sauce (optional).

9. Repeat again if possible.

10. Top with the remaining mozzarella and parmesan.

11. Cover with tinfoil and place in oven for 1 hour.

12. Take off tinfoil and bake another 10 minutes.

13. Remove from oven and let stand 15 minutes before serving.

14. Slice into squares and serve with donair sauce.

My first donair was in Halifax at a King of Donair. My girlfriend at the time told the guy serving us that I had never had a donair before – he gave us a smirk and proceeded to produce the greasiest, meatiest, sauciest donair to ever be made. I ate it all and had the meat sweats all night, ending with me passing out on the hill where the armories are. Good times.

- Paul (Hamilton, Ontario)

My buddy Todd and I started eating at the King of Donair on Quinpool in the mid-seventies (I'm not sure it was even called King of Donair then). At the time we sometimes got lamb meat and sometimes donair meat, so I think it was early in the game. We then made the switch to Tony's when Abe took over (Todd's mom knew Abe) and we became "regulars" most weekend nights (or mornings).

My story is ... we introduced donairs to a friend who worked at a ski resort in Maine (upon seeing the meat on the spit he said it must come from a mythical beast with large thighs and no bone to support it). On March Break ski trips we (still Todd and I, along with the wives) would load the van with the kids and we would stuff the front of the ski box on the roof with enough shaved meat to make a dozen or so larges (purchased unassembled). When we would get to the border, we had to explain to the kids that when the officer inevitably asked if we had any meat on board we would deny it, and explained to the kids, it's not meat ... it's donair!

When we would get to our condo at the hill, we would reheat the meat in a frying pan on the stove and invite some hill staff to the feast. We also would leave the condo door open so the aroma would waft down the halls driving all the other Nova Scotians nuts!

- Glenn (Halifax)

---

11 Sept 2001:

I was from the West Coast and living in A-Block (RIP) at the time, attending a 6-month course. After the events in NY that morning, class was cancelled for the rest of the day and we were told to call-in the following morning for further instructions. What else are a bunch of sailors to do with time off and a fist full of money in their hands? Yup....TO

THE PALACE!!

Many libations later, we make our way back to Stad around 0300 and stop at Venus (RIP) for a nightcap donair to go. Donairs in hand, we stroll through the gate and head up to our respective rooms; and this is where the story goes sideways.

Unbeknownst to us, hundreds of stranded airline passengers were now also being housed in A-Block, in every spare bed available. With me being a Master Seaman at the time, I had my own room which actually had three spare beds in it that were unused ... until now. I opened the door to my room, flicked on the light and tossed my donair on the desk as I tried to take off my shoes (remember, I'm hammered so it's not an easy feat). Then I hear it. Someone/thing from the other side of the room is asking me to turn out the lights and I finally clue in that there are three other people in my room who weren't there when I left several hours earlier.

I lose my shit and in my best R. Lee Ermey, I'm yelling at these three poor civilians (Dad and 11-year-old son combo and some rando dude) who just want to sleep, after what was probably a really shitty day. I realized they had no idea what I was saying (still hammered / not very coherent) but Dad gets up and puts out his hand to shake. I shake it, we go through introductions and I look at my small donair, sitting forlornly, waiting for me to eat it. The Dad and son were Scottish and the rando dude (Malcolm) was from Philly. We talked for a couple of minutes and I asked if they were hungry, which they were because all they had eaten were airline snacks and whatever food scraps were left over when they arrived at A-Block. I looked over at my donair and cut it up into three pieces and I let them feast. I wobbled back over to Venus for a pizza and drinks and brought it back for them so they could eat a bit more before we all went to bed.

By the time I recovered enough the next morning to open my eyes, they were gone and moved into various other accommodations which were probably much more habitable than my room and I never saw them again. Dad left a note thanking me for the donair and pizza.

That was the best donair I never ate.
- Belt Press from r/Halifax

I know a guy who shoved half a donair into the coin return slot of a payphone.
- Scott (Vermilion, AB)

Donair Heroes: Donair Supply (Wedding Band).

"So our band 'Donair Supply' started as a joke. Our old band 'Skully' played a lot in Ottawa at the Heart and Crown. The walk from the hotel to the bar had no less than 5 shawarma shops, and not a single donair joint. We felt we needed to make a donair name for the band to help represent Halifax. After a brief break-up, and a name change, we now are who we are. We actually prefer donair pizza after shows. It tastes much better when you eat it off the parking lot ground apparently....

"People constantly joke that we should bring donairs to our shows. We have about as much to do with donairs, as we do with Air Supply. We supply neither."

Until…

"A friend of mine in Florida had asked the band to deliver a donair to Florida, so I accepted the challenge. I had no idea what to expect. After browsing the U.S. border rules, I figured I was going to be put on a list for trying to smuggle meat into the country. Depending on your interpretation there wasn't a problem, or you are an international threat. (As much as a $10,000 fine if I try to sneak it in)

"I engaged with KOD via Twitter, and we had a laugh about the situation.

"So I head down to the King of Donair, and ask if they can help me with this mission. It turns out, this is a common occurrence. KOD will actually wrap all of the 'components' of the donair into separate containers.

"The key was the meat, which she gave me a heaping portion of. It was wrapped in tinfoil, and I shoved it into the appropriate-sized ziplock bag. The tomatoes and onions were not an issue. We both agreed that this was something that could be tossed. You can always just cut up your own when you get to the destination. The pita was another separate package. I was told to fry it in a pan with some water, and it would be just like new.

"Last but not least was the sauce. Well, it's not that easy getting the sauce on a plane. It's considered a liquid, so it would be a problem in my carry-on. The other thing that crossed my mind was how I would explain to a border guard what this creamy fluid was in a container. I know exactly what they would think it was, and well, gross. I wasn't a fan of this option. If I put in my luggage and it exploded, clothes would be covered in sticky garlic sauce, and I wouldn't have any way to clean it when I get there. It ended up not being a problem, because my friend down in Florida said he had some from his last trip home.

"Turns out that they now sell pre-packaged containers of sauce, so this is no longer an issue. (If you ever want to try this).

"So I get it all home, and have to figure out what I want to do. Do I put it in my luggage and not declare it, and face a possible $10,000 fine? Do I put it in my carry on, and claim it's my lunch? Or do I be honest?

"I get to the Halifax Airport, and I am not sure what is going to happen. We go to the American departures, up to the U.S. customs area. I am with my family, and we're

Members of Donair Supply eating a donair pizza off the ground. (Submitted by: Bruce Fillmore).

actually heading to Disney. Kids are with me, and I am not sure if I am going to make a huge mistake. You never know with these U.S. border guards.

"I walk up to the guy, and he asks if I have anything to declare. I have zero poker face, so I say, 'I have a donair.'

"He looks at me confused. I begin to explain the situation. He stops me and says:

"'It's OK man, I know what a donair is. I may be from Texas, but I live in Halifax. Let me tell you though, you chose the wrong donair. Have you been to the place up at the top of Larry Uteck? They are WAY better. Get the Super Donair there. It has pepperoni on it, and it is amazing.'

"That was when I knew that donairs had become the symbol of our city. I was never more proud. He told me to shove it in the bag, and have a good trip.

"Donair arrived in Florida, and my buddy was very happy. Donair Supply, Supplied."
- Bruce Fillmore

When I was in Barrie, Ontario, I stopped at a Ricardo's pizza. They had signs reading "authentic Halifax Donair" so I went in with my family. Ordered some donairs. Then the guy (owner I found out) asks me, "what do you want on it?" I said, "onions, tomato, mozzarella and extra sauce." Next thing I know he asks me, "what about cabbage?" I turned around and shot him a messed-up look and said, "umm no. Just the real donair toppings, thanks." He then started to persist that was normal. And so was lettuce... After some banter back and forth my kids thought I was going to get into a fight with the guy and went to go get my wife.

In the end I got a large donair with barely the amount of meat you'd get on a small. And no, I didn't get no f'n cabbage or lettuce.
- Dale (Brantford, ON)

Some years ago a friend learned of my trip to Halifax and asked for two donairs. I brought the extra-wrapped goodness back in a tied Sobeys bag via an overhead bin on a rather empty flight. Thank goodness; for when we landed and I opened the overhead bin.... The smell.
- Ian Collins

When I moved to Calgary in 2002 there really wasn't any place to get donairs. What they called donairs were not what I was used to. It had a plain garlic sauce and was more like a shawarma or a gyro. We tried donairs all over the city. Every time we heard there was a good donair somewhere we would make the trek, only to be disappointed. You know a donair is bad when you can't even stomach it drunk.

At this point I decided to learn how to make donairs from scratch. I researched and decided I would try the recipe as a surprise for my friend Sean's birthday. Sean was also from N.S. and a huge donair fan. For his birthday weekend a gang of us went backcountry camping in Kananaskis. We hiked in about 20 km to our campsite. We got settled and started to get ready for dinner.

There, in the majestic Rocky Mountains, I pull out the makings of donairs. We refried the meat over the open fire. They were amazing. It was an epic donair experience.
- KJ (Dartmouth, NS)

I once saw a kid in front of the QEH Commons entrance spiral a donair in foil directly into the path of a cyclist. It connected with the guy's neck and he went down in an explosion of nastiness.

I felt bad, but I did laugh.
- Jayson (Halifax, NS)

It's common knowledge to get donairs on a night of drinking on Whyte Ave. When I was 19 a friend invited me to his friend's birthday party. We started at Showgirls and soon after ended up at the birthday boy's house for the main party with roughly 10 people. Late night donairs are a thing, so around 3 or so... I remember someone ordering like, 8 donairs. I met a girl that night. We were chatting and making out almost all night.

When the donairs arrived, we snatched a couple and ate them above the kitchen sink. I basically inhaled mine, while she took her time. We giggled away at the sauce dripping into the sink and chunks of tomato, lettuce and onion. I licked a bunch of sauce off her chin, while she's damn near choking in laughter. I also snatched a bite of hers before wandering to find my drink.

This is where I lose memory, aside from the walk home, throwing up on the way, with my pal, as the sun was coming up. However, I was since told a week later or whatever, that I stole another donair and was seen squatting in the backyard behind some trees and bushes or something, with a smoke in hand chowing down. Once the story of the night circled my close group of friends, I was being called "donair sauce" for a little while.
- Kakarrot87 (Edmonton)

Buddy came to town from Calgary. We had drinks all night. Then we went to Pizza Corner, got donairs, and sat on the wall. Everyone walking by kept saying, "Welcome to Halifax" and he had no idea why. I said it's because "In Halifax we lean forward, not upright, so we don't wear the sauce."
- Val (Halifax)

A donair mother crosses a grassy field with her litter in The Motorleague's Hinterland moment.

Donair Heroes: The Motorleague

Moncton-based rock band The Motorleague made a parody of "Hinterland Who's Who" (Canadian public service announcements from the '60s & '70s that profiled Canadian animals) featuring the "Atlantic Lowlands Prairie Donair". They took partly unwrapped donairs and pulled them along the snow-covered forest floor with strings, showing their mating habits and even a litter of baby donairs following their mother. The narration says:

"Canada's lowlands are the home to one of the most beautiful and powerful members of the donair family, the Atlantic Lowlands Prairie Donair. The Atlantic Lowlands Prairie Donair, also known as the Eastern Canadian Gyro, is a small woodland animal, found in the frozen forests of Canada's barren East. For many years, the donair has been a protected species. However, it has made a successful comeback, after careful reintegration into the wild. The donair has always been sought after by trappers, for its lush outer coat, which is silver in colour. It was historically used by earlier settlers as a crude form of currency, as well as something to wrap sandwiches in…."

I was walking home to my girlfriend's house, very early morning and very drunk. Of course I picked up a donair on the way, as you do when you are drunk. I was locked out because she had not arrived home yet (I think … details are vague) so I hunkered down on the outside steps of the drugstore across the street to start enjoying my donair.

My useless drunken mitts start unrolling this thing on my lap. I grab the edge of the tinfoil and start unrolling, and it just rolls completely off my lap, and meat side down on the steps below. I don't even care, I'm wasted and starving so I pick it up best I can and get to eating. Fast forward to next morning/afternoon and I wake up with a weird grit in my teeth. In an instant it all comes flooding back to me that I ate a donair that had essentially rolled around in dirt and pebbles. I barely held it together that day, I was so disgusted with myself. From that point out, we lovingly referred to that moment as "Stair-Donair".
- Matthew Daye (Middle Musquodoboit,NS)

Bonita Chinchilla performing her donair number.

Donair Hero: Bonita Chinchilla (burlesque performer)

Bonita Chinchilla performed a donair-inspired number in which she undressed herself as a donair.

"I got the idea because I'm from Ontario, so I like to do things that are regionally specific now that I am here. My burlesque acts are usually goofy. I have a giant watermelon, a shark, an egg. One night I was looking at the King of Donair Instagram. I love their sense of humour, and I thought, why not Queen of Donair?

"I put it together with the song 'Teeth' by Lady Gaga, which fit because the meat in my donair act is my own flesh, and there is a line, 'take a bite of my bad girl meat', so it was perfect. It also just has the right attitude for a donair with extra sauce on the side.

"I have a giant silver cape that acts as my wrap and a small sparkling hat, both with the King of Donair logo on them that says 'Queen of Donair'. I open it to reveal balloon onions and tomatoes. I pop the balloons, and I have tomato pasties and a G-string, and as I roll around on my pita there is a small bottle of donair sauce which I use on myself, and then toss aside in favour of a giant extra sauce, big enough to dip my butt in. I pour it all over myself. (It's not donair sauce, though. It's off-brand Spectro Gel, because you can't wash costumes easily, so I don't really ever use food. I learned that from dumping coconut milk on myself previously)."

When I was just 19, I was downtown and getting hammered. I slept in my friend's truck in front of the Lord Nelson and woke up around 6 a.m. with a cold donair on my lap. I got out of the truck to get some air because I was beyond hungover and started to go to town on the donair. It starts to hit my stomach wrong and I start feeling very sick. A lady then walks out of the Lord Nelson with her kids and says something along the lines of 'This city is so beautiful! The people are amazing! I wonder what we're going to see today!' Just as she says that I, 10 feet from her, start puking my guts up into a bush. She looks over disgusted to see me holding a donair, puking with one eye open. I look at her and say, "Welcome to Halifax" and then puke again. She turns her family the other way and tries to shield their view.

Not my proudest moment but still makes me laugh.
- Anonymous

When KOD first opened in the '70s, my dad said that he drove by and saw there was a special of 2 donairs for X amount of money, can't remember the exact figure. He went in, got two of them, and went back to his car to destroy them. Now because these beautiful works of art are brand new to Halifax, my father attempted to eat it like you would eat any kind of wrap. He took a huge honkin' bite out of it and the ENTIRE contents of the donair ejected all over his lap, his car, etc. and my dad lost his marbles.

In his rage, he said he got out of the car, took the second donair and drilled it right at the window of KOD and drove off. He has since told me that he has a more loving relationship with donairs, but it was a rocky start.
- Anonymous

Donair Hero: Andrew Al-Khouri
Andrew Al-Khouri was a contestant on MasterChef Canada in 2015. His audition dish was a donair gnocchi that he now serves at his restaurant, aFrite. The story that follows, "The Night I Stumbled upon the Donair Omelette" appeared as a blog post on the Discover Halifax website:

One fond memory of my university days was a late-night stop at Pizza Corner, grabbing a grease-laden foil-wrapped donair, loaded with tomatoes, onions and that sweet sauce dripping at the bottom. I was walking home on a snowy sidewalk, when all of a sudden I caught an ice patch!

Wham!

I hit the ground, face planted and surely bruised. When I heard the relentless roar of my non-sympathetic friends, I hoisted up the donair, as if to sacrifice my body for this late-night culinary masterpiece.

With my ego bruised and elbows scraped, I made my way home to devour this thing. Oddly enough, I fell asleep before I was able to gorge myself.

This turned out to be a blessing in disguise. The next morning I had an Edison light bulb moment.

"What if I chop all this stuff up and add eggs?" I wondered.

It was so good! It was one of those times where all you can do is stand alone, smiling and giggling like a fool.

Here is the recipe:
1 left-over donair
3-4 eggs
2 Tbsp milk
Butter

Directions:
Chop up the donair into a large dice (bread, veggies, and meat). In a bowl, whisk eggs, milk, and add the chopped donair. In a medium saucepan over medium heat, melt the butter and add the donair-egg mixture. Once the egg has almost set, flip in half and turn off heat."

The victorious Nathan Richards. (From King of Donair's Facebook).

Donair Hero: Nathan Richards

The first donair speed eating contest took place on National Donair Day (December 8) in 2017. Nathan Richards took the crown, consuming a supreme donair (13 ounces of meat) in two minutes, 27 seconds. In 2018, Nathan Richards defeated Joel Hansen in the final, finishing this time in two minutes, 10 seconds.

I once took donair meat from Sicilian Pizza into the Quinpool Road McDonalds and asked them to make me a Big Mac using the donair meat. They said no, so I got a meatless Big Mac and reconstructed it on the front counter with my donair meat.
The MacNair was born.
- Sean (Halifax)

My first donair was in Halifax at Bash Toulany's. Bash, as my father put it, had one of the best and oldest recipes in Halifax. He'd been getting donairs from Bash since his teens. I was born in Halifax and raised in Lower Sackville. I cherished those trips to Toulany's, as my father passed in 2016, and our last trip there was in the early '90s.

As a raised Sackvillian I ate a lot of Jessy's, KOD, Pizza Nova, Greco Pizza, Sackville Deli Donairs, and their sub and pizza versions. I moved to Cambridge, Ont. in 2001 and could not find anything resembling a real donair here, aside from a 'skinny kit' that missed the whole experience, and was made in the United States. I got my dad to send me the recipe Bash gave him, the one without lamb, due to costs. And now when I am homesick I make my own donairs, and sauce. NEVER with lettuce but shredded mozza is a must. I get all my donair-inexperienced friends to enjoy the experience at least once. I made them in February to celebrate my dad's birthday.

Best food ever!

(Although my dad hated the garlic breath after. And yes, homemade leftovers can make a box of baking soda in the fridge tap out like a shop-bought one can).
- Jason M. Taylor

Donair Hero: Quake Matthews (rapper)

Halifax rapper Quake Matthews released his single "Down with the King", a tribute to King of Donair and Run DMC, in 2015. The track features music from the Run DMC classic. The video, which is filmed in the Quinpool KOD, features Randy and Tyrone from the Trailer Park Boys.

From the track:
"Cause I'm a true Nova Scotian
Wake up every Sunday drunk with donair on my clothin'
And every Saturday you know where I'm at
Like Randy with the cowboy hat
Yo, I'm down with the King (chorus)…
In my province
The donair is so iconic
But other places never seem to have the right toppin's
Pardon me, I don't really mean to start it
But you put tzatziki on it, homie, I don't even want it, nah"

From Quake Matthews' music video *"Down With the King* (2015)".

First time visiting home after moving to Calgary and went out for drinks, etc. Had to have a donair late at night, but for some reason I was like an amateur and forgot how to eat it. Ruined a nice winter jacket, but damn did I laugh and loved being home.
- Crystal (Calgary, AB)

Two decades ago, a girlfriend and I once got a super donair from Louis Gee's in Corner Brook. The thing was huge, the size of an infant, and we ate it over the course of a week or so. I'll never look at one of those things the same ever again.

I just remember it sitting in one of those big Pyrex pans in its foil, the glory of it, the smell, the absurdity, the extremes of young love.

Every time I go home I invariably go to Louis Gees for their large honey garlic fingers with extra sauce... And think of my buddy.

Ahh, to be young again.
- Anonymous (Newfoundland)

American Hunter: In 2018, Brad Fenson, of Ardrossan, Alta., had his recipe for wild game donair published in *American Hunter*, the official journal of the NRA. He recommends using elk, moose or venison and says they work well because they're lean, but says that triple grinding, or emulsifying them in a food processor is key to getting the right texture.

Donair Hero: Heather Nolan
(Creator of "Halidip")

"Donair dip, or 'Halidip', was the result of a conversation my husband and I were having on the drive home one day, and while the two of us can have horrible memories, both of us remember the exact location on the Bi-Hi we were when the recipe was born (102 outbound, right around the Dunbrack exit LOL).

"My husband and a co-worker had been chatting earlier in the day about the possibility of a donair soup, and when he told me about it, my first thought was GROSS! (We now know that not only is donair soup possible, it's quite the opposite of gross). The seed had been planted and my mind started thinking of my donair recipe and what I could create as a play on the donair. Dip! I've never met a hot dip I haven't loved, and by the time we got home I had ALL the ingredients in hand to create the recipe bouncing around in my mind. Basic, unhealthy, but delicious.

"The experiment was a huge success so I rushed to post the recipe on my old blog that night, I was so excited about it. And it got basically no traffic. It quickly became a hit with my neighbourhood inner circle, but that was it. If I recall, it was close to a year before the recipe got picked up somewhere and all of a sudden, I had massive traffic to both my blog and my blog's Facebook page. The recipe was being recreated at local restaurants and pretty much any potluck in the city. What I loved most were all of the comments I was getting on the recipe from around the world, grateful for an easy recipe for a taste of Halifax.

"My blog is no longer active, but I've had a few people track me down online looking for the recipe, which is really flattering, I'm just happy so many people enjoy it."

HaliDip Recipe
1 lb lean ground beef
1 tsp dried oregano
1/2 tsp cayenne pepper
2 tsp paprika
2 tsp garlic powder
1 tsp onion powder
1/2 tsp each salt and black pepper
1 8-oz container regular cream cheese
1/2 cup shredded mozzarella
1 cup donair sauce
1 tomato, seeded and diced

In a bowl (truth be told, I did this in a non-stick frying pan before putting it on the heat), mix together the ground beef and spices and blend well, really, really, really knead it together well. Then fry up the mixture, breaking it apart with a wooden spoon as it cooks. You don't want any chunks of meat too big... it has to remain scoopable.

While the meat is browning, make your donair sauce, and then in your cooking dish (a 9-inch glass pie plate or small casserole dish) mix together the cream cheese, donair sauce and shredded mozzarella.

Once the meat is cooked and well-browned, use a slotted spoon to transfer the meat (but not the grease) to the cooking dish and fold it in to the cream cheese mixture. If you won't be eating it until later, you can cover and put in the fridge at this point. When it's go-time, just pop the dip into a preheated 350-degree oven and cook it for 20 minutes.

Sprinkle the diced tomatoes (and some minced onions if you like) over the top of the hot dip and serve!

One time I walked across a frozen lake in a storm after a party, and took refuge in a local pizza shop. On the counter was what looked like a football wrapped in tinfoil. It turned out someone ordered an extra extra large donair and never came for it. I gave the kid 5 bucks for it and stuck it in my coat.

The thermal contents of that pita kept me warm and safe for the next hour of storm walking, and was still warm when I opened it up and ate half of it.

Some donairs are bigger than others, but God has a plan for those ones.
- Kyle (Sackville, NS)

401 East

In 2007, the province of Nova Scotia created a campaign encouraging displaced Maritimers to move home. One of their controversial ads was a video based on the show "Intervention" where a young man was confronted by friends about his "Delusional Calgaria" (the mistaken belief that one must move to Calgary in order to be financially successful). The same campaign also included billboards spread around Toronto that resembled directional road signs. They simply said "401 East: Donairs" with an arrow pointing east.

Donair Hero: Neil MacFarlane

Neil used to have a Facebook page ("Donairs I Have Known") where he reviewed more than 50 donairs around Halifax. He also single-handedly conquered the Bash Toulany "Rumble Challenge" Party Donair, and survived to tell his story:

Running at the bargain price of $9.99 plus applicable taxes, I expected something about the size of two large donairs as I naively placed my order on the phone. I should have recognized the insidious laughter on the other end of the line as an ill omen. Hindsight truly is 20/20.

Upon its arrival at my door, I knew I was in for the culinary challenge of my life. The delivery man, looking fresh from a stay in Dorchester Penitentiary, cradled what appeared to be a small child under his arm, wrapped in a comically oversized paper sack.

He rocked it lovingly, as if it were his only son, and demanded his cash. Upon payment, he handed me the bundle, and I realized that most meals I had eaten in the past did not require two hands to comfortably carry anywhere and that no meal I had ever eaten by myself caused a sudden strain on my shoulders and forearms as this one did. The delivery man grinned oddly at me as he left as if he knew what was to transpire.

I prepared for battle by removing my pants and shirt, revealing standard donair eating garb: stained, off-white tank top, broad hairy shoulders, dishevelled hair and faded boxer shorts. Eating something like this was a near erotic experience, so being half-naked was an essential requirement.

It was then my meal's turn to be undressed, and as I worked through the packaging, I became concerned that there was no donair to be had at all, only tinfoil. Instead of the standard one sheet of aluminum to swaddle the donair, there was at least half a roll of foil armour protecting the precious meaty womb of this beast.

In a scene reminiscent from *Aliens*, the foil suddenly split and the bulk of the steaming mass splayed open as if I had cracked its ribcage, revealing the spiced vital organs of this xenodonair specimen.

I took a moment to admire its glossy finish, to stare at the pits and crevasses in the meat, to note its pitted textures and to observe the eddies and swirls the vapour from this fiery feast created. I knew that it was time to begin.

As with any piece of food put before me, my North End upbringing dictated I should eat it as quickly as possible, lest some undeserving greaseball break into my house and try and wrest it from me.

How was I to know that the training that had raised me so well in the past would be my own worst enemy on this occasion?

After mowing through a good pound and a half of donair flesh with frightening alacrity, a sickening horror crept over me.

I am still unsure if it was the skilled method of meat stacking, or if the veritable bucket of donair sauce on this behemoth was causing hallucinations, but it was as if the meat was somehow regenerating, as there hardly seemed to be a dent in the mound before me.

I struggled to convince myself that the growing mass in my gullet was in fact consumed donair, but the sprawled carnage before me seemed unfazed, almost taunting me; again, I questioned if the sauce was causing hallucinations, this time auditory in nature.

I immediately downed a Molson Canadian in an attempt to steel my nerve before I delved back into the fray.

In my childhood, I had a fiery temper. When sufficiently provoked, I would lose my mind and go into a trance-like state, seeing only red and blocking out all but the most primal of urges and instinct, succumbing to fits of rage and violence.

It had been many years since my last tantrum, but on this night, I managed to again summon that sub-human power to my aid, as I once more entered a world where there was nothing but myself and my enemy, and I swelled with a desire to obliterate it at all costs.

My next cogent thought was that of extreme digestive discomfort.

I looked about, bewildered, to see I was still in my living room, still in front of this unholy donair decadence.

I was thoroughly drenched in a horrific cocktail of cast-off donair sauce and my own sweat, my shirt so saturated that I at first thought that I had been shot in the upper-chest at close range and was bleeding donair sauce instead of blood.

I clumsily lurched forward and gaped at the plate before me on the table, and saw I was nearing the home stretch. In the seemingly impervious donair meat armour, chinks appeared, revealing white patches of soft pita below.

With the spirit of a madman, I laid into the weakened donair, now eating with a disturbing sense of urgency. I heard what I presumed were my bowels, straining and wheezing like a train-wreck. My roommates would later claim it was, in actuality, a loud truck outside the house, but I know what I heard in those dire moments.

Eating with both hands, I forewent my regular breathing schedule in favour of increased access to my stomach, running a dangerous risk of drowning in the donair sauce that was literally dripping from these last few morsels of mayhem.

And in an instant -- they were gone. Save a few tooth-sized chunks of brown meat flecks, there was only the pita left.

I should have known it was a trick.

Upon lifting the flat husk that remained, I came to realize there was much more than pita bread at work here.

This was a pita that had been sitting in a veritable lake of MSG and grease for some 30 minutes at this juncture, absorbing all the heart-stopping, artery-clogging agents from the donair meat that once called this tarp-like piece of bread home.

I began to question if this pita was in fact not a living creature, as when I tore off a hunk to stuff into my face, it bled strange orange goo, akin to blood, only runnier.

With my goal in sight, I mindlessly drove each fist-portioned slab of this repulsive leavened obscenity into my mouth, swallowing without chewing as needed to expedite the macabre task, as if my very life depended on it.

I was dizzy, bloated and perspiring profusely. Convinced that my gut was about to rupture, I envisioned my poor sainted mother, having to part with her only son in a shameful closed casket ceremony, as the funeral home would not be capable of sufficiently repairing the ghastly damage caused when the entire lower half of my body exploded as a result of devouring this goliath of grease.

Just as I thought I was about to cross that tenuous threshold and enter the Valley of Death, I looked down ... and the donair was gone.

Nothing remained except tinfoil shreds, a befouled plate and the few remaining tatters of my dignity.

Man had triumphed over donair, and the idea of celebrating crossed my mind for about a nanosecond before massive internal hemorrhaging and spasms took centre stage and I collapsed into the fetal position on the carpet floor, twitching slightly.

I lay there for an eternity, trying to make sense of what had just transpired.

I'm not a religious man, but I knew at that moment, without a shadow of a doubt, that there existed something in this world outside of what we can see and sense, a being of incomprehensible power and reign capable of altering the lives of all mankind with a mere whim.

And his name is Bash Toulany.

Antacidote

"They say that they originated in Greece, but I just got served one by this Lebanese guy's niece. You won't find them in fancy restaurants, but when it's 3 a.m. it's the only thing I want."
– Chad Hatcher, "Campfire Story 3: The Donair Song"

The donair is a proud member of the doner kebab family, with Greek lineage, Lebanese influence, Nova Scotian incubation, and Albertan liberation. Whether you're eating a big 'ol bloated donair from Randy's Pizza on Agricola Street in Halifax or a Hawaiian Chicken Donair from Donair Town on Robson Street in Vancouver, you are participating in a Canadian tradition.

I wasn't sure how to wrap this up, so I ordered a large donair from my local shop and unwrapped it onto a plate. There it sat before me, an impossible pile of meat, defying all demarcation.

What is this thing, how do I eat it, and what does it say about national identity? Broken down to its most basic components, it is Albertan (or P.E.I.) beef shaped by Greek chefs into an old Anatolian recipe.

It is Saskatchewan wheat, transformed into Arabic bread by Lebanese bakers.

It is Greek tzatziki sauce, adapted to Maritime taste buds, and inspired, perhaps, by the sweet and sour success of Chinese Canadian cuisine.

Who knew that a region known for lobster and bagpipes could have been such fertile ground for multicultural ingenuity?

The donair lying belly up before me betrayed the shift from its European intentions to North American excesses.

I picked away at the strands of factory meat blend, and wondered how far we've come from the original recipe. I decided to eat half of the donair with tzatziki sauce, and half with donair sauce, hoping to derive inspiration from this juxtaposition of past and present, east and west.

The tzatziki was bright and fresh, and I could picture my donair with a squeeze of lemon, a sprinkle of parsley, and even a bit of crunchy lettuce, wrapped up tight on a hot summer day.

But then I delved into the sweet sauce, and I was transported to a midnight kitchen party, scooping out the last remnants of sauce with my fingers, drunk and sticky and surrounded by friends.

The secret ingredient: nostalgia.

While not everyone subscribes to the concept of the Halifax-style, I would argue that it is this interplay of spicy and sweet that makes the Canadian donair what it is. It is the gastronomic expression of Canadian multiculturalism; a symbol of unity in a country so big and diverse, it shouldn't work – but it does.

The donair is indigenous to both Nova Scotia and Alberta, two provinces that get along like oil and water. The regions are so dramatically different and yet so many young Maritimers have found themselves full of piss and vinegar in the land of milk and honey!

Sometimes this sauce threatens to separate, but if you mix it lovingly, and don't overwork it, it can harmonize into a sweet powerhouse of a condiment.

Are you ready for the answer to the riddle? What is the unifying concept of every donair, the one thing that all donairs have, and that you can't add or subtract without losing the donair?

The answer: Love.
I'm so sorry. I forgot to hold the cheese.

So, to the Halifax puritans: let's accept our fellow Canadians with open pitas! I would love to see a Winnipeg Fat Boy Donair, a Pacific salmon bannock donair, or a Sugar Shack pancake donair. I think we can have fun with it, while, at the same time, protecting our proud tradition.

We are all part of one great nation united by gravy and cheese curds, butter and raisins, sweet sauce and spicy meat. Our differences are what make us stronger. Just trust in the alchemy.

ACKNOWLEDGEMENTS

Everyone knows it is hard to write a book, but it is even more difficult than I could possibly have imagined and I have learned so much. Thank you to MacIntyre Purcell Publishing for taking a chance on me, and providing the opportunity I've always dreamt of. Vernon Oickle and Rick Conrad have been there for me the whole journey. Thanks for your mentorship!

Thanks also to Jennifer Crawford, Andy Hay and Omar Mouallem for your written contributions to the book. I am honoured.

This project has come a long way since 2015 when I was originally trying to make a YouTube show. When my producer went AWOL (apparently to the UK) and my camera man retreated to Cape Breton with all the footage, I put the donair on the back burner and stewed for a while on how to proceed. When I did return to the subject, it was with a vengeance. My father, who has become quite the community researcher in his retirement, brought me along on trips to the Halifax Central Library and the Nova Scotia Archives, introducing me to resources I had not previously considered. I would like to thank him (and Mom!) for their guidance and support – proofreading, forwarding articles and helping with genealogy.

A grand gesture of gratitude is owed to my wife, Cindy, for her endless support. It isn't easy to live with an obsessed foodie, yammering on about the crisis of lettuce or the etymology of Greek words, and it certainly isn't easy to live with a writer plagued by all the usual clichés: imposter complex, self-sabotage, banging head against wall, procrastination (that never seems to involve household chores) and existential dread. She has been my harshest critic and my biggest cheerleader. To my Side Dish: the road trips to weird places and the donairs that didn't sit well - thank you for your patience, support and love.

There is one obvious person without whom I would never have written this book: the inventor of the donair, Peter Gamoulakos. His culinary ingenuity, at a time when Canadians were slow to appreciate anything that was "different" or "foreign", has created a symbol of regional pride that has influenced the culinary identity of a whole nation. To all of the Greek and Lebanese immigrants who experienced hardship, who came to Canada, who built communities and bolstered economies – Canada would be lesser but for your impact and culture.

I couldn't have written this book without the co-operation of the many families that were involved with the donair in its early history. I would like to extend a very gracious thank you to the Gamoulakos family for your co-operation in this project.

Thank you to Peter and Jim Dikaios for answering my email queries over the years, and to John Kamoulakos for speaking with me. Thank you to Abe and Leo Salloum for helping me with the Tony's story, and to Tony Nahas for helping me with the Mezza story. You've all helped me untangle a lot of loose ends!

Thank you to Omar Mouallem – Edmonton's foremost donair scholar – for your Albertan perspective and expertise.

Thank you to Chawki (Charles Smart) El-Homeira, Peter Garonis, Jaco Khoury, Abe Toulany, Mike Klayme, Jack Toulany, Gus Tectonides, Nick Giannopoulos, Dimitri Neonakis, Chris Jebailey, Josh Robinson, Moe Akkad, Mike Nicoletopoulos, Geoff Mockler, Travis Milos, Gus Anbara, Troy Power, and Yuri Airapetian for taking the time to talk with me, which for some of you involved lengthy interviews!

Thanks to Bassil Sleiman, Marc-André Chartrand, Tibet Arikan, and Wajdi Chehimi for taking the time to help me learn your stories, and allowing me to use your photos. To Krista MacLeod-Tingley and Aaron Tingley: much thanks for your help with the Mr. Donair story, and providing photos of the plant.

Thank you to Mike Whittaker of Grinner's Food Systems for helping with the New Brunswick story.

Thank you to Dr. Nick Nicholas for your help with linguistics and Greek language web sites, even though you will probably never see this book in Australia.

Thank you to Glen Petitpas, Waye Mason, Murray Wong, Allan Milisic, Brad Delorey, Mario Eleftheros, Cailin O'Neil, Neil MacFarlane and Scott Bossert for your help with this project.

Thank you to Chad Huculak for the comics; Souper Duper Soup, Andrew Al-Khouri and Heather Nolan for sharing their recipes; Jennifer Bain, Matt Dagley, Amy Jo Ehman and Tim Krochak for generously sharing their photographic contributions.

To all: a heartfelt thank you and I hope you enjoy this book.

SOURCES

(1) Spurr, Bill. "Donairs in his future: Famous chef Bourdain puts delicacy on list of must-try foods." *The Chronicle Herald*. (November 13, 2014).

(2) Toole, Brittany. "Nova Scotia donairs are infiltrating the country and we couldn't be more thrilled." *The Chronicle Herald*. (July 14, 2017).

(3) Brown, Chuck. "The sweet sauce makes this Turkish, or Greek – or Lebanese delight a Maritime mystery donair love affair." *New Brunswick Telegraph Journal*. (October 16, 2002).

(4) Petitpas, Glen. Glen Petitpas's Homepage. (https://www.cfa.harvard.edu/~gpetitpas/Links/Donair.html)

(5) Gold, Jonathan. "The year in food: changing tastes." *Los Angeles Times*. (December 27, 2009).

(6) Pantronite, R. and Raisfeld, R. "King Bee Will Introduce New York to the Donair (Think Acadian Gyro)." *Grub Street (New York Magazine)*. (April 9, 2015).

(7) Pace, Natasha. "First ever donair crawl hits Halifax." *Global News*. (August 15, 2015).

(8) Patil, Anjuli. "Donair study approved by Halifax council in official food consideration." *CBC News* (online). (October 21, 2015).

(9) Ramsden, James. "Did Kadir Nurman really invent the doner kebab?" *The Guardian*. (Oct. 28, 2013).

(10) Miller, Kenneth. "Archaeologists Find Earliest Evidence of Humans Cooking with Fire." *Discover Magazine*. (December 16, 2013).

(11) Mott, Nicholas. "What Makes Us Human? Cooking, Study Says." *National Geographic*. (October 26, 2012).

(12) Nasrallah, Nawal (2007). *Annals of the caliphs' kitchens: Ibn Sayyār al-Warrāq's tenth-century Baghdadi cookbook*. Brill. p. 40.

(13) Gannon, Megan. "Ancient Greeks Used Portable Grills at Their Picnics." *Live Science*. (January 8, 2014).

(14) Ayto, John. *The Diner's Dictionary: Word Origins of Food and Drink*. Oxford University Press: October 18, 2012. (p118).

(15) Seidel-Pielen, Eberhard. "Döner fever even in Hoyerswerda." *Zeit Online*. (May 10, 1996).

(16) Nail Tan (1990). "Kastamonu'nun ünlü yemek, yiyecek ve içecekleri" [Famous dishes, food and beverages of Kastamonu]. *Türk halk kültürü araştırmaları* [Turkish folk culture researches] (in Turkish). Vol. 1. Ankara: Halk Kültürünü Araştırma Dairesi [Department of Folk Culture]. p. 109 f.

(17) Ed. Artemis P. Simopoulos, Ramesh Venkataramana Bhat. *Street Foods*. The American Journal of Clinical Nutrition, Volume 75, Issue 2, February 2002, Pages 337–338 Karger Medical and Scientific Publishers. Basel, Switzerland.

(18) James, Alice. "Memories of Anatolia: generating Greek refugee identity." *Balkanologie*. Vol. V, No. 1-2 (December 2001).

(19) Ventiera, Sara. "The Ultimate Guide to Vertical Street Meat, the OG Fast Food." *Zagat*. (October 31, 2017).

(20) "Souvlaki: The historical dish of the Greek and the foreign root of the name". *To Pontiki* (Online). (April 19, 2019).

(21) Tzianidis, Nikos. "Prohibitions in Greece: From the 'skirt' of Pangalos to the anti-smoking law." *Ethnos*. (December 2, 2019).

(22) Kakissis, Joanna. "Don't Call It 'Turkish' Coffee, Unless, Of Course, It Is." *The Salt*. (April 27, 2013).

(23) "The Gyro, a Greek Sandwich, Selling Like Hot Dogs." *New York Times*. Sept. 4, 1971, p. 23.

(24) Segal, David. "The Gyro's History Unfolds." *The New York Times*. July 14, 2009.

(25) Berry, Donna. "Gyro meat puts Mediterranean cuisine on the map." *Meat + Poultry*. (May 10, 2018).

(26) Class, Skye. "Is a Kapsalon the Best or Worst Invention from Rotterdam?" *Perceptive Travel*. September 7, 2018.

(27) María del Mar Calderón. "The story behind the first tacos árabes in Puebla". *Eat Mexico*. (November 30, 2017).

(28) Arnold, Lita. "'Donairs' find a firm foothold". *Chronicle Herald.* (1978).

(29) Chimbos, Peter D. "Greek Canadians." *The Canadian Encyclopedia* (online). June 12, 2008. (Updated by Celine Cooper, September 12, 2019).

(30) Maroudas, Spiro C.A. "Greek Immigration to Montreal in the 50s and 60s." *Park Extension Historical Society.* (March 22, 2016).

(31) Nosowitz, Dan. "Meet the 81-Year-Old Greek-Canadian Inventor of the Hawaiian Pizza." *Atlas Obscura.* (June 4, 2015).

(32) Funk, Cory. "'They stole the recipe, which is good': How the Fat Boy burger became a Winnipeg icon." *CBC News* (online). (November 3, 2019).

(33) "Halifax's Pier 21 designated national museum." *CBC News* (online). (February 7, 2011).

(34) Atwood, Haleigh. "Building Community with Coffee". *Halifax Magazine.* (April 29 2019).

(35) Dempsey, Amy. "Saga of Halifax's first donair resembles Greek wrapsody". *The Star.* (December 6, 2015).

(36) Van Horne, Ryan. "You Don't Have to Call Him Tony". *My Halifax Experience.* (June 22, 2016).

(37) Honorary Degree - Bassam Nahas. Saint Mary's University (Online News). (April 22, 2016).

(38) Erksine, Bruce. "Donair maker oozes success." *The Chronicle Herald.* (October 5, 2006).

(39) Fida, Kashmala. "King of Donair feels some online burn for MAGA-style hat giveaway at Grande Prairie opening." *The Star* (Edmonton). (July 25, 2018).

(40) "Bonté foodservice donair meat sales % by region." Retail Donair Category. Bonté foods. (June 18, 2015).

(41) Ward, Rachel. "King of Donair sues Alberta shops ahead of Calgary expansion". *CBC News* (online). (July 5, 2016).

(42) Klingbeil, Annalise. "King of Donair looking to open permanent Calgary location after huge demand at pop-up shop". *Calgary Herald.* (March 7, 2016).

(43) Mouallem, Omar. "The Donair Wars: Halifax's favourite street meat conquers Alberta." *The Walrus.* (June 2015).

(44) "New Economic Realities: Canada enters a new era characterized by economic uncertainty and growing globalization." *Canada: A People's History*. (Based on the award-winning CBC TV series that tells Canada's story through the eyes of the people who lived it). (2001).

(45) Klinkenberg, Marty. "Canada's oldest Muslim community finds solidarity in Edmonton." *The Globe and Mail*. (February 2, 2017).

(46) Mouallem, Omar. "Will The Real Burger Baron Please Stand Up?" *Swerve*. (February 5, 2013).

(47) Potkins, Meghan. "Q & A: The three investment bankers behind Calgary's definitive donair rankings." *Calgary Herald*. (February 27, 2015).

(48) Mouallem, Omar. "Street Treat: Why the donair is the staple of late-night dining." *Swerve*. (November 20, 2015).

(49) "Management of the Risks Related to Consumption of Donairs and Similar Products (Gyros, Kebabs, Chawarmas and Shawarmas)." *Health Canada*. (2008).

(50) Moore, Oliver. "Group aims to beef up safety rules for donair meat." *The Globe and Mail*. (July 3, 2008).

(51) Lambie, Chris. "N.S. Donairs: They induce babies, upset tummies and make us homesick." *The Chronicle Herald*. (2004).

(52) "Businessmen take beef over donairs to N.S. small claims court." *CTV News Atlantic* (online). (July 31, 2017).

(53) Alhmidi, Maan. "How the donair, with its Greek origins, became Halifax's official food." *The Guardian: A Saltwire Network Publication*. (June 17, 2019).

(54) "Products". *Athena Donair Distributors* (website).

(55) "Truro-based company Trucorp Investments earns prestigious recognition." *SaltWire Network*. (April 23, 2017).

(56) Markel, Howard. "How Dr. Kellogg's world-renowned health spa made him a wellness titan." *PBS News Hour* (online). (August 18, 2017).

(57) Denker, Joel. *The World on a Plate: A Tour Through the History of America's Ethnic Cuisine*. Bison Books (October 1, 2007).

(58) Jones, Sonia. "From Culture to Cultures: True Tales from the Yogurt Queen of Eastern Canada." *Los Angeles Times*. (July 19, 1987).

(59) Druker, Julie. "Fresh take on the history of Ontario garlic." *Frontenac News.* (September 9, 2015).

(60) Atwood, Haleigh. "Where I work: Fancy Lebanese Bakery." *The Coast.* (April 12, 2018).

(61) Sevunts, Levon. "Moncton bakery gives free pitas to Syrian refugees." *Radio Canada International* (online). (February 2, 2016).

(62) "Fancy Pokket Corporation: Perfect Pitas". *Industry Today.* Vol. 5, Iss. 1. (2009). (Published online on July 26, 2016).

(63) Nuetzenadel Alexander and Frank Trentmann. *Food and Globalization: Consumption, Markets and Politics in the Modern World.* Bloomsbury Publishing. (May 1, 2008).

(64) Cyprus Pita (from Cyprusisland.net).

(65) Chattman, Lauren (2011). *Bread Making: A Home Course: Crafting the Perfect Loaf, From Crust to Crumb.* Storey Publishing. p. 202. (2011).

(66) Morgan, Jordi. "An Open Letter to Mayor and Council on the Donair Debate." *Jordimorgan.com.* (October 27, 2015).

(67) Whitehouse, Jordan. "Millennials in Franchising: Mezza Lebanese Kitchen." *Franchise Canada Online.* (June 7, 2017).

(68) "Bash Toulany's Fine Foods: About Us". *NSlocal.ca.*

(69) DeMont, John. "A litigious history of the donair." *The Chronicle Herald.* (September 23, 2019).

(70) Buote, Melissa. "The life and times of Pizza Corner." *The Coast.* (February 20, 2014).

(71) Boon, Jacob. "Slice of history: Pizza Corner's untold stories." *openfile.* (October 17, 2011).

(72) "King of Donair to leave Halifax's pizza corner." *CBC News* (online). (January 19, 2012).

(73) "Municipality says Pizza Corner signs in downtown Halifax need to be taken down." *Global News* (online). (September 7, 2018).

(74) "Mharbe Rafih" (Obituary). *InMemoriam.ca.*

(75) Damascus shuts its doors." SaltWire Network. (April 21, 2016).

(76)   "Reborn pizza restaurant to open in Truro." *SaltWire Network*. (March 1, 2018).

(77)   Vellend, Eric. "Chef's Showcase: Baked peppers stuffed with rice, tomatoes & herbs." *The Star*. (May 7, 2011).

(78)   Follert, Jillian. "Donair craving is a thing: Fans say Oshawa spot is doing the meaty Maritime speciality right." *DurhamRegion.com*. (October 24, 2019).

(79)   Warhaft, Marion. "Turkish delight: Pembina takeout offers some of the best donairs, shawarmas around." *Winnipeg Free Press*. (November 4, 2013).

(80)   Melnychuk, Mark. "Prairie Donair founder has his sights set on a cross-Canada franchise." *Regina Leader-Post*. (December 14, 2019).

(81)   Booth, Dawn. "Best Food: Best Donair." *Your McMurray Magazine*. Vol. 7-4. (October 21, 2019).

(82)   Saunders, Allison. "How Fort Mac does donairs." *The Coast*. (December 11, 2014).

(83)   Anthony, Kristyn. "Local businesses forced out in Esquimalt Township's purchase of building." *Victoria News*. (January 12, 2018).

(84)   Groff, Meghan. "Remember This? The 20,000 people buried near Pizza Corner." *Halifax Today*. (June 3, 2019).